The Giant Leap

A Chronology of Ohio Aerospace Events and Personalities

1815-1969

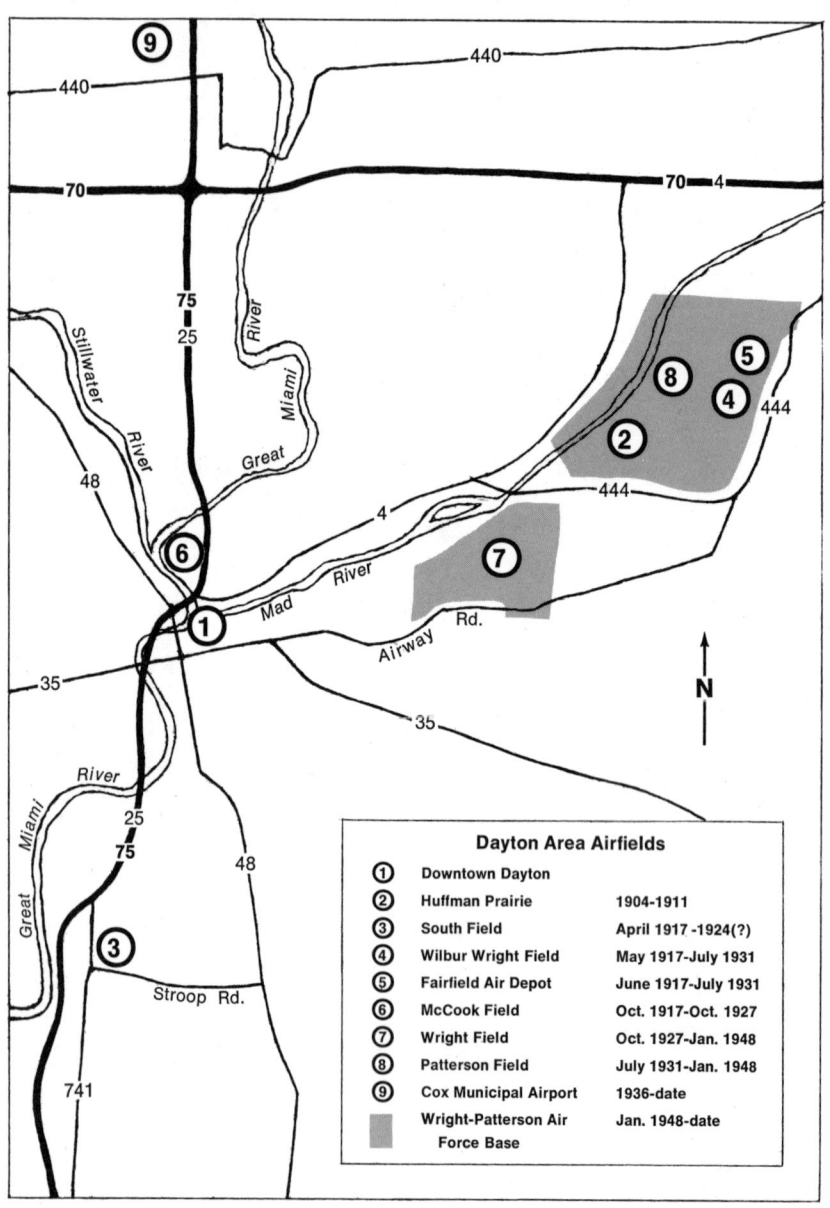

The Giant Leap

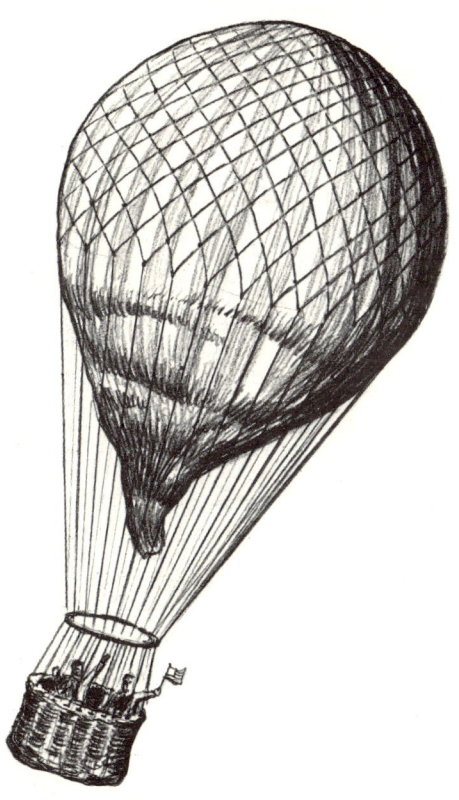

A Chronology of Ohio
Aerospace Events
and Personalities

1815-1969

Tom D. Crouch

The Ohio Historical Society

Columbus, Ohio

Copyright © 1971 by The Ohio Historical Society

Preface

Accomplishments are the progeny of diverse parents . . . sometimes perseverance and hard work, sometimes dreams and opportunity, sometimes circumstance and serendipity. In the accomplishment of the flight of man, the parents could count each of these elements in his family tree. But perhaps the most important ingredient was inspiration. First the flight of birds, then the flights of the gods of mythology, and finally the flights of the aviation pioneers have inspired man to rid himself of the shackles of gravity and find freedom in the realm of flight.

Two centuries ago, in a hot air balloon, that dream was finally realized. With the airplane, that reality has become practical and useful . . . in less than a lifetime. The fences confining man's imagination have been shattered and the walls confining his person to one planet have been breached. He has begun to explore his universe.

The state of Ohio has been singularly involved in the flight of man. I know I can speak for many of my fellow enthusiasts in confirming the influence of the pioneers in general, and the Wrights in particular, on the spectacular successes in aviation and in space that our generation has witnessed. That type of inspiration will continue to be the motivating force that drives men toward capturing their dreams and searching for their destiny.

This chronology of the part played by Ohio and Ohioans will contribute to that inspiration. It is a useful text for the serious student or historian and an entertaining diversion for those of us who just like flying.

Neil A. Armstrong

Introduction and Acknowledgments

The absence of a comprehensive survey of the history of aeronautics in Ohio is striking in view of the fact that the state was both the birthplace of flight and a center of early developments in the field. Although other states have taken the lead in detailing the aerial achievements of their citizens, Ohio has largely neglected its rich aeronautical heritage. This chronology is not an attempt to provide the complete story of aviation in the state, but to sketch a background which may serve as the basis for more specialized studies in this vital phase of Ohio's technical history.

Emphasis of the *Chronology* is on the balloon ascents of the 19th century and on the early years of heavier-than-air flight. Although this period is particularly rich in primary source materials, it remains the least known to either the specialist or the general reader. It was the feeling of the author that these materials deserved a more detailed presentation than was necessary with later periods. This early period has a distinctive flavor and contains events and personalities which are clearly the product of the Buckeye environment. Also, the history of aviation since 1930 has been covered in detail in other works.

The skills and assistance of a number of individuals have proved invaluable in the preparation of this chronology:

Daniel R. Porter, director of The Ohio Historical Society, suggested the need for such a document and offered constant encouragement and support. Marilyn G. Hood, editor of special publications of the Society, edited the book, and Daniel H. Stouffer, Jr., was the designer.

Royal D. Frey and the research staff of the U. S. Air Force Museum, Wright-Patterson Air Force Base, provided many of the photos of military personnel and equipment. Stanley Vaughn and Ernie Hall, two of Ohio's pioneers of flight, answered a seemingly endless series of questions and opened their extensive private photo collections for the author's inspection. Dr. Edward Korn, whose name appears in this chronology more than once, provided photos on his own activities as an exhibition pilot. Dr. George J. Ruppel offered data and suggestions.

Michael Ballen, who served as student research assistant, demonstrated outstanding patience and considerable skill in examining contemporary newspaper and magazine sources. Charlette Robinson willingly typed the many revisions of the *Chronology*. The final manuscript was typed by Patricia Davis.

Tom D. Crouch
Supervisor of Education
The Ohio Historical Society

Chronology

July 4, 1815—Ohioans were introduced to flight by a Mr. Gaston, who released a large hot air balloon "decorated with an American Coat of Arms, descriptive of the present times" at a fireworks exhibition in Cincinnati. Even though this early ascent was unmanned and served only to attract customers for the fireworks, it did excite much interest and comment in the city.

June-October 1834—A. Mason, a Cincinnati mechanic, constructed an "aerial steamboat" in which he hoped to "ascend beyond the surface of this earth and navigate the air by the force of steam." The craft consisted of a standard small boat hull, covered with silk in order to reduce its weight. A lightweight steam engine turned four rotating shafts which were fitted into a frame attached to the hull. Four "wings" similar to helicopter blades were placed on top of each shaft. The leading edge of each "wing" was raised so that as the shaft was rotated, the "wings" served as airscrews. When Mason placed his machine on public display in August 1834, it drew much favorable comment from the Cincinnati press. Although the inventor presumably attempted to fly the craft, no record remains of such an effort. Even though the "aerial steamboat" was grossly underpowered, it demonstrated a basic understanding of the aeronautical principles known at that time.

November 20, 1834—Thomas Kirkby, a native of Baltimore, Md., announced that he would attempt the first manned balloon ascent in Ohio in a standard silk envelope with a gas capacity of 10,000 cubic feet. The ascent was to be made from a specially-constructed amphitheater on Court Street in Cincinnati on November 27. Payment of an admission charge of 50 cents would allow the spectator to view the inflation of the balloon and the release of small trial balloons to test the direction and velocity of the wind, and to enjoy the fine "band of music" hired by the aeronaut to entertain the visitors during the two and one-half hour inflation period.

November 27, 1834—Thomas Kirkby's gas generating apparatus—a series of casks filled with water and iron scraps to which sulfuric acid was added to produce hydrogen gas—proved faulty, postponing the ascent for one day.

November 28, 1834—When Kirkby's equipment failed again on the second attempt, a mob of angry citizens threatened to destroy the aeronaut and his balloon. They were dispersed, but returned the following day inspired by a "determination to level every thing connected with it [the balloon]." The timely arrival of Mayor Samuel Davies and 19 officers saved Kirkby from a fate not uncommon for 19th century aeronauts. The ascent was postponed indefinitely to give Kirkby an opportunity to rebuild his generator and check the equipment.

December 15, 1834—Having completely rebuilt the gas generator with the aid of several "scientific gentlemen," Thomas Kirkby became the first man to fly in Ohio. Traveling east from the Cincinnati amphitheater, the aeronaut passed over the Ohio River and landed on the farm of one Samuel Riley, near Williamsburg in Clermont County. The trip covered 31 miles in slightly less than an hour.

December 27, 1834—Following a rapid ascent, Kirkby circled Cincinnati prior to disappearing behind a low range of hills on his second successful balloon trip. The flight ended near Milford, some 13 miles from the city. Although local newspapers carried an account of a Kirkby ascent from Louisville on March 7, 1835, nothing is known of his later career. In view of this obscurity, it is probable that he adopted a less hazardous profession soon after leaving Cincinnati.

April 8, 1835—Richard Clayton, a young English watchmaker and recent immigrant to Cincinnati, became the second man to take to the skies of Ohio. His balloon, *Star of the West*, was larger than Kirkby's and he made more thorough plans for the ascent. To attract spectators, Clayton announced that he would present the first parachute drop west of the Alleghenies. The owner of the dog which he dropped to safety in a basket was later offered $100 for the animal, but declined it with the comment that he believed the creature was now popular enough to be elected Vice President. Clayton continued his voyage for an unbelievable 350 miles, eventually landing in Monroe County, Va. This flight, which set a world record for distance traveled in a free balloon, brought the aeronaut's name to the attention of aeronautical enthusiasts in America and Europe. Clayton's success was so striking that the editor of *Western Monthly Magazine* suggested that he undertake a voyage to the moon in *Star of the West:*

> . . . he may easily engage the services of a few schoolmasters and schoolmistresses . . . in order to teach our language to the benighted people of that strange land . . . instruct the poor lunatic heathen how to erect splendid dwellings, and magnificent churches, and furnish them with the best lawyers, doctors, schoolmasters, and devines. . . . Excellent books might be prepared for the instruction of the lunarians . . . [and] their language doubtless needs to be corrected.

May 13, 1835—Richard Clayton narrowly escaped disaster on his second flight in Cincinnati. Moments after he left the ground serious leaks appeared in his balloon, forcing him to land on a neighboring roof.

July 4, 1835—Four thousand Cincinnatians witnessed Clayton's departure on his second successful flight. He had hoped to reach the Atlantic Coast but was forced down near Piketon, Ohio, by bitter cold which turned the balloon fabric "as hard as wood." Letters and newspapers which he had planned to deliver in the East were sent to the post office at Waverly, from where they continued their journey by more conventional means.

May 1, 1837—On this occasion Clayton, unable to inflate his balloon fully, discarded all excess weight including the basket, ballast, and equipment, as he hoped to make a low altitude ascent seated on the netting which hung from the gasbag. Still unable to ascend above ten feet, the aeronaut cut away the lower, uninflated portion of the gasbag with a pocketknife and was able to rise to a "reasonable altitude" over Cincinnati.

July 4, 1838—Richard Clayton went aloft from Cincinnati with an unidentified "lady companion." This was the first recorded flight of a woman in Ohio.

Summer 1838—The nation's second astronomical observatory was constructed at Miami University, Oxford, Ohio. John W. Scott, professor of mathematics and natural philosophy, installed a stone pier to accommodate a small transit telescope. A wooden shed built around the pier to protect observers was dismantled and used as firewood by students during the winter of 1838-1839. The stone and the iron mounting for the telescope can still be seen near the entrance to Bishop Hall on the Miami campus.

1838—Elias Loomis, professor of mathematics and natural philosophy at Western Reserve College, founded Ohio's first permanent observatory at Hudson. This structure consisted of a central revolving dome and wings which housed astronomical instruments and a small library. The observatory was equipped with both transit and equilateral telescopes and an astronomical clock, all of which Loomis had purchased in London. With these instruments Loomis and other Western Reserve astronomers were able to make a number of significant scientific contributions. The building is now the second oldest observatory still standing in the United States.

October 1839—The Cleveland *Herald* advertised a "Great Discovery!" in "Aerial Navigation!!" For $5000 James C. Patton promised to deliver express mail to New Orleans in 15 hours. When questioned by the New York *Commercial* as to Patton's ability to operate such a delivery service, the Cleveland editor was unable to locate the aeronaut.

July 1842—Having acquired additional experience in a number of ascents in Kentucky and West Virginia, Richard Clayton provided the citizens of Columbus with their first opportunity to witness a balloon flight. The ascent was made from an open area near the State House. Clayton's record of this flight is typical of many offered by aeronauts of the period:

> The movement of the balloon was so steady that no sensation of motion was experienced; the earth appeared to gradually fall from my feet, and the spectators to dwindle into dwarfs and blend at last into masses. . . . A number of persons on horseback endeavored to keep up with me, who, together with their horses, resembled the toys of children moving with snail-like velocity. . . . After feasting for a few minutes upon the beautiful view beneath me, I turned my attention to the balloon, and arranged the various articles in my little car, so as to have no confusion at the time of landing. This being done, I took some refreshments, which an old acquaintance and intimate friend had provided for me. . . . Five minutes of six, gained the altitude of two miles; looked back to see Columbus, but it was lost in the hazy vapor. The thermometer now stood at 38°; a great quantity of water poured down upon me from the neck of the balloon. This water was taken into the balloon in the form of vapor, when the gas was generating; and afterwards, when it was exposed to extreme cold, condensed and fell in copious showers of rain upon me. Being drenched with water . . . I felt extremely chilly and rather sick at the stomach; the sickness was occasioned partly, perhaps, by inhaling a goodly quantity of hydrogen gas. A tea-spoonful or two of brandy, and a little excellent cake, prepared by a fair friend of mine, restored me to my proper feelings. . . . My landing was effected at twenty minutes after six o'clock, . . . on the farm of Mr. Seymour, five miles east of Newark, and thirty-eight miles east by north of Columbus.

November 9, 1844—John Quincy Adams dedicated the cornerstone of the Cincinnati Observatory. The campaign to construct an observatory had followed a series of lectures on astronomy delivered by Ormsby MacKnight Mitchel in 1841-1842. Interest in the lectures was so great that Mitchel suggested a public subscription to raise funds for the purchase of a telescope and the construction of a suitable building to house it. The Munich firm of Merz and Mahler constructed the 11 and one-half inch refracting telescope which was installed in the observatory on Mt. Adams upon completion of the building in 1845. By 1872 it had become apparent that the site of the observatory was useless because of the smoke discharged by factories which had sprung up in the area, and the telescope and other instruments were transferred to their present site on Mt. Lookout. The observatory is part of the University of Cincinnati.

July 4, 1851—John Wise of Lancaster, Pa., made a Columbus ascent as a member of a traveling show organized by John M. Kinney. Based in Columbus, Kinney's Mammoth Pavilion toured Ohio each summer, offering a variety of entertainment to residents of the Buckeye state. On this occasion, Wise's balloon *Ulysses* was launched from an enclosure which Kinney had constructed on the corner of Broad and Seventh streets. Wise traveled six miles to the south, landed without incident, and returned to the city that evening. Wise, like Clayton, offered a description of the capital city:

> ... the city of Columbus lay out before me like a well defined map, and the meandering Scioto looked like a way worn pioneer who had reached the furthermost point of his career. The National Pike shot its straight white line eastward until it was lost in the far distant east. ...

One of the most distinguished aeronauts of the pre-Civil War period, Wise had made his first ascent at Philadelphia in 1835. He was responsible for a number of technological improvements in free ballooning, the most important of which was the ripping panel. This was a section of fabric lightly stitched to the side of the gasbag, with a cord attached to its upper end. Upon landing, the aeronaut would give a healthy tug to this line, which was always dyed red, ripping this section from the bag and allowing the remaining gas to escape. Prior to the introduction of the ripping panel, aeronauts were often dragged over the countryside by a half-empty balloon acting as a sail. The dragline, a length of rope used to control altitude and, to some extent, direction of travel, was also developed by John Wise.

August 15, 1851—John Wise made an ascent at Zanesville in the *Ulysses*. The voyage which lasted for an hour and three-quarters, covered a distance of six miles.

September 5, 1851—John Wise made a second Columbus ascent, this time with his wife and young son. After a 35 minute flight, the aeronaut landed to allow his passengers to leave the car. Reascending, he landed near Blendon Corners, some ten miles from Columbus.

October 2, 1851—Thousands of spectators assembled in Springfield to witness John Wise ascend in his "fine looking balloon." Following a "successful and beautiful ascension," the aeronaut traveled to a woods eight miles northeast of Columbus, where he was able to anchor the balloon in the top of a tree. He estimated he had covered 65 miles in only 58 minutes.

October 1851—John Wise and his family traveled with the Kinney show to Cincinnati. The aeronaut described the Queen City as seen from the basket of the *Ulysses* as resembling a "frog with its hind legs drawn apart." Spring Grove Cemetery had the appearance of a ribbon tied in a "true lover's knot." He descended, after an eight mile flight, on the farm of a Mr. Cummings in Springfield township.

October 6, 1851—"Prof." Ira J. Thurston completed the first balloon ascent in Cleveland. A New Yorker, Thurston was one of the most popular balloonists of the period. For this flight he used his balloon *Buffalo*, starting near the foot of Erie Avenue and landing in East Cleveland. Thurston made a number of ascents in northern Ohio, Michigan, and New York. On the morning of August 16, 1858, having landed in Adrian, Mich., after an ascent there, Thurston climbed on top of his partially deflated balloon in order to force the remainder of the hydrogen from the gasbag. This was not an uncommon procedure for aeronauts operating without ripping panels. On this occasion, however, the balloon, free of the weight of the ballast and passengers, rose a second time, overturning as it ascended. Thurston was able to cling to the gasbag and, seated on the balloon valve, disappeared over Lake Erie. Evidently he held on until the valve broke under his weight, dropping him to his death.

1852—During the summer John Wise traveled with the Kinney show throughout Ohio, making ascents at the various stops. He lectured on the art and science of aerostation prior to each ascent.

June 3, 1852—John Wise made an ascent from Portsmouth in the face of an approaching thunderstorm. Once aloft, he was caught by the storm and carried in its wake to Pt. Pleasant, Va. Wise was able to remain aloft by jettisoning all of his ballast, and he landed safely near a cabin in the woods. The next morning he packed his gear and conveyed it to a nearby river landing, where he was able to catch a steamboat to return to Portsmouth.

June 10, 1852—During an ascent from Chillicothe, John Wise rose to an altitude of one mile and remained aloft for 45 minutes. The voyage was cut short when the netting connecting the gasbag and basket fouled, causing the balloon to swing back and forth violently. Prior to his descent, however, Wise obtained a good view of the prehistoric earthworks in the Chillicothe area:

> I noticed a dozen towns in view but my eyes were once arrested by a sight between the city and the river; I noticed some figures that seemed to be printed in the soil. . . . As I saw it, the outlines [of the earthworks] were to some extent obscured and broken by different objects.

June 17, 1852—John Wise made a short ascent from Circleville.

June 24, 1852—During a Lancaster ascent, Wise got a bird's-eye view of the Scioto Valley:

> ... the prospect was grand and extensive; at an altitude of 4000 feet there was brought into view Columbus, Zanesville, Circleville, Newark, Chillicothe, Logan, and innumerable little villages. The canal shown like a silver telegraph wire strung wavelike over the landscape. ... As I lowered within hailing distance, loud salutations reached my ears: "You look like Gabriel." or "Come down, come down." My ignoring of the appeal seemed to increase the infection and before I finally landed, I had hallooed myself hoarse.

The 16 mile flight ended on the farm of William Bowlin in Marion Township, Hocking County.

July 17, 1852—John Wise ascended in the *Ulysses* at Mansfield in a 30 mile an hour wind. At an altitude of 11,000 feet the balloon ". . . was distended to her most pompous dimensions, smoking at the mouth like an overcharged steamer."

July 31, 1852—Wise traveled 30 miles to Minerva, Ohio, during his second flight from Massillon.

August 7, 1852—Wise offered a graphic portrait of the Akron area as seen from a balloon floating over the city:

> ... the world disclosed myriads of beautiful objects. Akron with its surrounded scenery, seemed as though it grew spontaneously and rapidly out of the earth, whilst the country immediately underneath appeared to be sinking away deeper and deeper as the balloon rose. ... The long straight lines bounding the townships, peculiar to the topography of Ohio, converging in the distant horizon, gave the vast surface below the appearance of a great city—the township centres looking like squares and prominent spots in the great rural thorougfare [*sic*]. Lake Erie lay quietly with its glossy surface in the northern vista, its bright surface marred in several spots, by smoke from steam boats. ... I made a sudden descent a short distance beyond the village of Tallmadge, five or six miles from Akron. ...

September 15 16, 1852—A series of Cleveland ascents closed the Ohio career of John Wise. The aeronaut had long been convinced of the existence of a low altitude current of air blowing from west to east across the Atlantic, and hoped to utilize this "jet stream" to facilitate a transatlantic crossing. On June 27, 1859, Wise with William Hyde, O. A. Gager, and John LaMountain ascended from St. Louis in a balloon which they hoped could conquer the Atlantic. They traveled across Lake Erie, where they found it necessary to jettison the mail they carried, and were forced to land near Henderson, N. Y. The group's transcontinental plans were forgotten in the heat of the arguments which followed this flight.

During the opening months of the Civil War, John Wise volunteered his services to the President and was appointed chief balloonist for the Union Army in Virginia. However, the observation balloons which Wise prepared for use at the front were destroyed in transit to Bull Run.

On September 28, 1879, John Wise ascended with George Barr, a bank teller, from Lindell Park in St. Louis, and subsequently was lost over Lake Michigan.

October 23, 1852—William Paullin, an aeronaut who had previously competed with John Wise in a Philadelphia balloon race, ascended at Zanesville. Advertising that he would return to the exact spot where he went aloft, Paullin hired Elijah Ross, a local gunsmith, to follow the balloon, grab a line dropped from the basket, and tow him back to Zanesville.

June 23, 1853—William Paullin made an ascent from Sandusky.

August 28-29, 1855—The irate citizens of Milan destroyed the balloon *Elephant* when it failed on two separate occasions to ascend as advertised.

August 1855—Timothy Winchester ascended before a large crowd at Norwalk and disappeared over Lake Erie.

September 24, 1855—Eugene Godard, a famous European aeronaut, went aloft from Cincinnati with his wife and J. C. Belman, "balloon editor" of the Cincinnati *Daily Gazette*, in the balloon *Ville de Paris*. The trio traveled to Hamilton with a light snack of turkey, chicken, duck, bread, cakes, wines, and cordials.

October 1, 1855—Godard and Belman, with William Hoel, a river pilot; William Latham, general agent for the Great Miami Railroad, and William Crippen, a reporter for the Cincinnati *Daily Times*, made a second ascent from Cincinnati. Caught in a thunderstorm, the men crashed near Waynesville, Ohio. Hoel received three broken ribs; the others escaped with minor injuries.

October 2, 1855—Samuel Winchester made a flight from Milan to Hudson.

July 1856—Delegates to the Democratic National Convention in Cincinnati found it difficult to concentrate on the problems of selecting a presidential candidate. Local newspapers reported that most preferred to watch the ascent of Prof. Pussey at Mme. Tournaire's Circus.

October 29, 1857—Eugene Godard and his wife carried P. W. Huntington and R. H. "Rocky" Thompson aloft from the Capital City Premium Fair and Exhibition Grounds in Columbus. Rising over the crowd, the aeronaut suspended himself head down from a rope attached to the basket. The party landed that evening near Reynoldsburg. A second ascent, during which Mme. Godard was to go aloft seated on a horse in a specially-built large basket, was postponed when the city was unable to furnish a sufficient quantity of gas.

November 4-9, 1857—The Godards remained in Columbus in the employ of Search's New Orleans Minstrel Show. They hoped to make a series of flights in the 36,000 cubic foot balloon *Canada*, but inclement weather forced postponement day after day, until the Godards found themselves destitute. A group of 36 local citizens gave a benefit dinner at which $89.50 was raised so that the Godards were able to continue their tour.

July 5, 1858—The Godards returned to Ohio for a second tour of the state. The first ascent of the 1858 season was made in Cleveland where the aeronaut went aloft with a Mr. Eberman, Dr. H. A. Ackley, and Dr. Sterling. The city donated the gas for this ascent which was part of the official Fourth of July celebration.

October 1858—An unidentified lady balloonist staged a "daring exhibition" at the Cambridge Fair.

October 18, 1858—The celebrated balloon race between Prof. John Steiner and Eugene Godard was held in Cincinnati. A minor riot began when the race was delayed for a few minutes, but both aeronauts were able to ascend without damage. The balloons remained quite close together for the first three-quarters of an hour, enabling the aeronauts to converse freely with each other. Following a minor collision, however, the balloons drifted apart. They traveled a distance of 250 miles, Steiner descending near Sandusky and Godard a few miles to the south in Monroeville. Steiner was declared the winner and "world champion aeronaut." J. C. Belman, whose balloon had been launched with the other two, landed near Glendale, only a few miles from Cincinnati. Belman had earlier claimed that he would reach the North Pole and "return to Cincinnati by way of the Equator." While most of the state's newspapers commented enthusiastically on the possibility of long range balloon voyages, the Cleveland *Leader* referred to the enterprise as "humbug" and a "waste of effort."

May 1, 1859—A traveling "professor" named Wilson announced in Dayton that he would offer lectures on ballooning and the natural sciences, as well as slide talks on his world travels. Wilson constructed a small hot air balloon of muslin coated with glue and ochre, to which a clothes

John H. Steiner is forced to leap from his balloon during an attempted aerial crossing of Lake Erie. Steiner was later the winner of Cincinnati's great balloon race in October 1858.

Frank Leslie's Popular Monthly, January 1877

basket was attached with rope to serve as a balloon car. The professor claimed that the Rothschild family had invested some $15,000,000 in his aeronautical experiments, and he refused to peril their money (or his life) in a personal demonstration of the airworthiness of his craft. Jacob Sellers, an employee of Frank Welty's Ice Cream Parlor, volunteered to go in his place. Lines were attached to the makeshift basket so that the novice aeronaut could be retrieved should he change his mind once airborne. Large holes which had been accidentally burned in the muslin bag during inflation were tied off with twine but they reopened several hundred feet over the city, necessitating a rapid descent.

May 10, 1859—A Dayton teenager named Brown made a second ascent in Wilson's balloon. The crew handling the lines was inexperienced and hung on too long, sending the craft into wild gyrations as it rose over the city. Brown, terrified by the rolling and pitching of the craft, made most of the trip standing up clinging to the gasbag, but was eventually able to bring it to a safe landing. The citizens of Dayton, now openly critical of "Prof." Wilson and his wild claims of aerostatic experience, forced him to leave town.

Summer 1859—David McFarland Cook of Mansfield designed and constructed an unsuccessful flying machine. Cook, a locally famous inventor, had earlier patented a device to extract beet sugar and a mysterious "electro-magnetic machine." The exact nature of Cook's *Queen of the West*, as he termed the flying machine, is not clear. Early newspaper reports suggested that Cook was building an airship, combining a balloon bag with a steam engine. Cook himself, however, claimed that it was a heavier-than-air craft and was not powered by steam. While the inventor constructed the craft in a secluded barn near Mansfield, he kept reporters and curiosity seekers at a distance, so that no report of the machine's appearance is available.

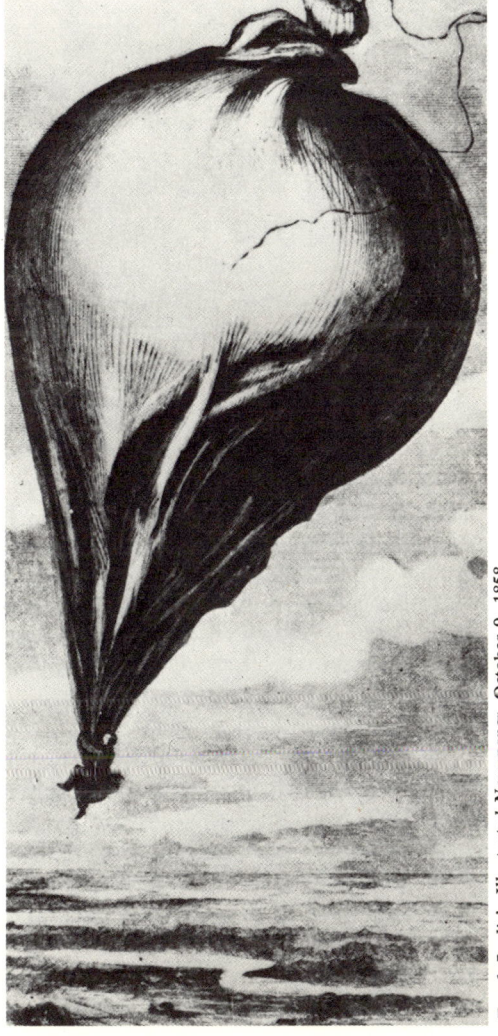

"Prof." Ira Thurston floats to his death on August 16, 1858, over Lake Erie. On October 6, 1851, he had been the first man to make a flight from Cleveland.

Frank Leslie's Illustrated Newspaper, October 9, 1858

"Prof." Lynn and a companion await rescuers in Lake Erie following a Cleveland flight on July 4, 1859.

July 4, 1859—"Prof." Lynn and an unidentified companion were forced down in Lake Erie following a Cleveland ascent. The two aeronauts waved flags and congratulated one another on a "successful" flight until rescuers arrived.

September 2, 1860—William Shotts made a Cleveland ascent. He escaped with an injured ankle when the balloon burst at an altitude of 160 feet and he fell to the ground.

September 8-14, 1860—Charles C. Coe and Prof. Q. L. Andrews of New York brought the largest balloon in the world to Cleveland. When fully inflated the giant aerostat stood 208 feet tall and was 118 feet in diameter. The gasbag contained 1,736,000 cubic feet of hydrogen. The balloon car, 39 and a half feet in diameter, was furnished with Brussels carpet and seats which rivaled those of a fine hotel. The balloon was far larger than the other giants of the period, including Thaddeus Lowe's *City of New York* and Felix Nadar's *Géant*. Coe intended to take the balloon to St. Louis for flight tests prior to attempting an Atlantic crossing, but the ultimate fate of the craft is unknown. The two aeronauts did, however, bring a smaller balloon in which they hoped to make a Cleveland ascent. This aerostat was caught in a sudden storm and destroyed on the ground before the flight could be made.

Harper's Weekly, June 18, 1859

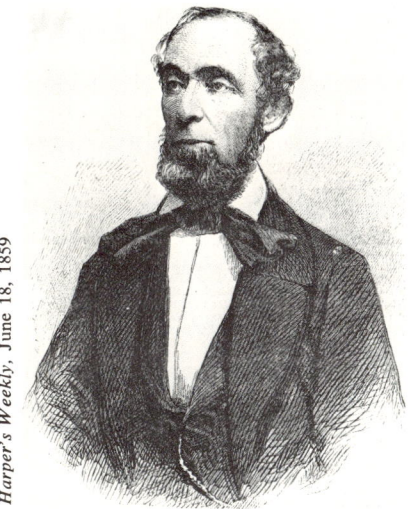

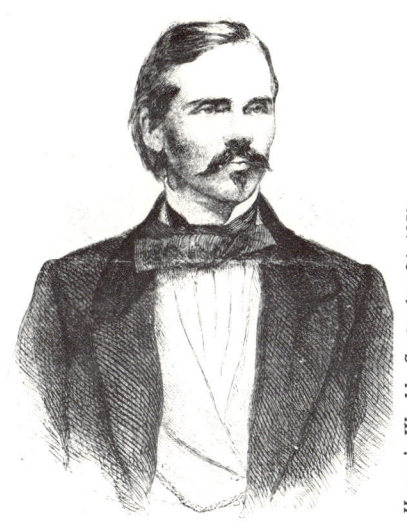

John Wise, one of the nation's foremost aeronauts.

Harper's Weekly, September 24, 1859

Thaddeus Sobieski Constantine Lowe.

April 20, 1861—Thaddeus Sobieski Constantine Lowe made his first Ohio flight. Born in Jefferson Mills, N. H., Lowe had become interested in ballooning as a boy. He made his first ascent in a homemade balloon during a visit to Ottawa, Canada, in 1858. In 1859 he constructed the large *City of New York*, later known as *Great Western*, and prepared to cross the Atlantic by air. The project failed when it became apparent that the balloon would not develop sufficient lift to undertake such a voyage. Joseph Henry, secretary of the Smithsonian Institution, suggested to Lowe that he acquire additional experience in long range balloon travel by making a flight from an inland point to the East Coast. Accepting Henry's advice, Lowe journeyed to Cincinnati with the balloon *Enterprise*, determined to complete an aerial voyage to the Atlantic Coast. Able to interest Murat Halstead, editor of the Cincinnati *Commercial*, in the project, he received extensive free publicity. The flight began shortly after 2 a.m. April 20. Traveling about 1000 miles, Lowe descended near Unionville, S. C., at 1 p.m. the same day, having nearly accomplished his goal of reaching the Coast. The unwelcome "Yankee" visitor was unceremoniously housed in the jail until rescued by local officials who recognized Lowe from newspaper pictures. Arriving in Columbia, S. C., on his journey north, Lowe was arrested and placed in jail as a Yankee spy a second time. He was released when the mayor of Columbia recognized him as the famous aeronaut who had planned to cross the Atlantic. Lowe returned with the *Enterprise* to Cincinnati by train on April 26.

May 8, 1861—Thaddeus Lowe, with Jacob C. Freno, W. W. Ware, and Junius Brown, ascended from the grounds of the Commercial Hospital in Cincinnati. Their intended journey to Washington, D. C., was interrupted by a landing near Bethel, Clermont County, where Freno and Brown departed to return to the city. Lowe and Ware continued, but were blown over Lake Erie to Hamilton, Ont. There Lowe made a number of profitable ascents in honor of the 42nd birthday of Queen Victoria. He then continued to Washington by train. Lowe soon after was appointed chief of the Balloon Department, which had been created to serve the Union Army in Virginia; he served with distinction until 1863.

July 4, 1862—F. H. Westbrook died as his balloon fell to earth from an altitude of 500 feet during an ascent from Sparta, Knox County. The balloon fabric, which was rotten, "burst in pieces and fell to the earth, killing the reckless navigator." B. L. Swetland, a resident of Sparta, took up a collection for the aeronaut's wife and children.

September 13, 1864—William Shotts made a "beautiful ascension" from Columbus in his balloon, *General Grant*.

Spetember 15, 1864—A "Prof." Brooks advertised a moonlight ascent from Columbus, but was forced to cancel the performance when the drain on the municipal gas supply threatened to plunge the city into darkness. The spectators, convinced that they had been duped, attacked the aeronaut and destroyed his apparatus.

July 4, 1866—John Steiner returned to Ohio to give a Fourth of July exhibition in Cleveland. The city council, which paid for the gas used in the ascent, was reported to have considered its money well spent.

1867—John Nelson Stockwell, a mathematical astronomer living at Brecksville, developed calculations which permitted him to measure precisely the motions of the moon. Stockwell's interest in astronomy had begun when he had observed a lunar eclipse as a boy. Fascinated by the sight, the young Stockwell studied almanacs and taught himself algebra, geometry, and some calculus. Soon after he published his first book, *The Western Reserve Almanac of the Year of our Lord, 1853*, in 1852, he accepted a post as a computer with the U. S. Coast Survey and the U. S. Naval Observatory, Washington, D. C. Stockwell was appointed first professor of mathematics and astronomy at the new Case School of Applied Science in 1881. The astronomer's chief contributions to science were his computations of lunar eclipses and his work on the effect of the moon on the tides.

Washington Harrison Donaldson, the "man on the flying trapeze."

Amick: *History of Donaldson's Balloon Ascensions, 1875*

March 28, 1872—Washington Harrison Donaldson, the original "man on the flying trapeze," performed before a large crowd in Columbus. A former circus acrobat, trapeze artist, ventriloquist, and magician. Donaldson made his first public ascent in 1871 in Philadelphia. The daring nature of his aerial activities, which usually included a trip aloft on a trapeze bar rather than in the conventional balloon basket, guaranteed maximum attendance at a Donaldson ascent. Throughout his career as an aeronaut, Donaldson was a member of P. T. Barnum's troupe of traveling performers. He often preceded the circus, drawing crowds and distributing advertising. During the Columbus ascent, he had risen some 75 feet when his balloon struck a smokestack, knocking off a number of bricks and ripping the gasbag, after which he "dropped rapidly into an adjoining yard."

April 22, 1872—Following a Chillicothe ascent, Washington Donaldson was unable to deflate his balloon properly and was dragged over the countryside "through a stream of mud and water" by the half-empty envelope which acted as a sail.

April 28, 1872—Donaldson's balloon struck a building during his second Chillicothe flight. He continued to rise, "tearing off sixteen layers of brick. [He was] instantly hurled against a second chimney, tearing a number of bricks from that also." In his landing, the aeronaut struck a tree, careened over a stone fence, and bounced three times across an open field before coming to rest.

May 11, 1872—Donaldson journeyed from Portsmouth to Zaleski, ripping his gasbag in landing.

May 20, 1872—During an Ironton ascent Donaldson gained altitude too rapidly, causing the hydrogen to expand at such a rate that the balloon ripped the netting to which the trapeze bar was attached. "This caused me to feel very uneasy, and on that account the voyage was devoid of the pleasure to me that usually attends the trip," he reported.

May 25, 1872—A second Ironton ascent by Donaldson was cut short by high winds.

May 28, 1872—Donaldson continued his tour of southern Ohio with an ascent from Gallipolis.

June 1872—Washington Donaldson traveled 100 miles on his second flight from Gallipolis.

June 24, 1872—After a performance on the trapeze bar for the citizens of Columbus, Donaldson "flew" to Mt. Sterling.

October 14, 1872—Donaldson carried a party of reporters on a flight from Cincinnati to Butler County.

October 19, 1874—The world's first aerial wedding was performed in a balloon taken aloft by Washington Harrison Donaldson. Miss Elizabeth Walsh, the bride, was a featured equestrienne in Barnum's Roman Hippodrome act, and the bridegroom, Charles Colton, was also "of the great show." In addition to them, the Rev. Howard B. Jeffries and two attendants were carried aloft for the ceremony. The takeoff was witnessed by a large crowd of spectators gathered in Cincinnati's Lincoln Park. Donaldson made four more Cincinnati ascents in October 1874, carrying a number of passengers including one party of admiring young ladies.

July 4, 1875—Samuel Archer King flew from Cleveland's Public Square to Birchard's farm near Mantua in Portage County.

One of Donaldson's most spectacular stunts—taking aloft the aerial wedding party on October 19, 1874.

Frank Leslie's Illustrated Newspaper, November 7, 1874

July 15, 1875—Washington Donaldson and Newton S. Grimwood, a reporter for the Chicago *Evening Journal*, made an ascent from Barnum's Chicago Hippodrome. The two proceeded across Lake Michigan where they were presumably lost in a storm. Grimwood's body was recovered some time later, but the remains of Washington Harrison Donaldson were never found.

1880—James Gordon Bennett, the New York publisher, offered Thomas Alva Edison $1000 "to make experiments in the direction of flying." Edison claimed to have constructed a helicopter, but no records or photos exist of such a device. He also constructed an internal combustion engine which he felt would be light enough, yet produce sufficient power to raise the craft. Edison called a halt to these experiments when the engine, which was fueled with ticker tape made into guncotton, exploded, injuring the inventor and an assistant. A French engineer circulated an engraving purporting to be "Edison's Flying Ship," but this picture probably bears little relation to Edison's vision of a flying machine.

1881—Worcester R. Warner and Ambrose Swasey established a machine shop in Cleveland. The men, both of whom were experienced amateur astronomers, combined their hobby and profession by producing a refracting telescope in their machine shop in 1881. The workmanship and quality of this instrument secured for the new company its first major telescope contract, for a 36 inch refractor for the Lick Observatory on Mt. Hamilton, San Jose, Calif. Following the successful completion of this project, Warner and Swasey constructed the 40 inch telescope for the Yerkes Observatory, Williams Bay, Wis., which is still the largest refracting telescope in the world. In 1916 the company completed work on the 72 inch reflecting telescope for the Dominion Astrophysical Observatory of Canada at Victoria, B. C. In addition, Warner and Swasey produced the telescopes for Perkins Observatory, owned by Ohio Wesleyan University at Delaware, and the Case School of Applied Science, Cleveland. Other astronomical instruments produced by the company have included transits, meridian circles, zenith telescopes, and quality optical finders.

July 4, 1881—Charles H. Grimely made an ascent from Columbus in his 22,000 cubic foot balloon *Columbus*. On this flight he traveled some 40 miles southeast of Columbus to Rushville in Rush Creek Township, Fairfield County.

July 6, 1882—Accompanied by S. J. Ficklinger of Columbus, Charles Grimely ascended from the capital city. After traveling northeast, the two descended on the academy lawn in nearby Central College.

September 1, 1888—Prof. Bassett thrilled a large crowd at Cedar Point with a balloon ascent and parachute jump from 500 feet.

1892—Burr Frank Barnes, a Circleville inventor, patented a design for an airship with electrically powered rotors, but the airship did not reach the stage of actual construction.

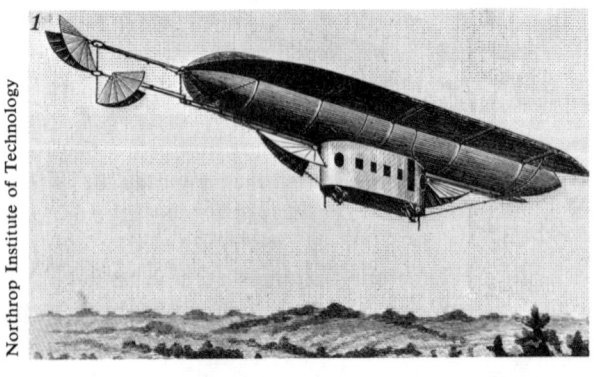

A patented airship designed in 1892 by Burr Frank Barnes, a Circleville resident. The machine was not constructed.

Walter Wellman, Ohio-born journalist, polar explorer, and aeronaut, in 1906.

1895—Daniel Caulkins, a Bryan, Ohio, physician, published a book, *Aerial Navigation*. In it the doctor proposed the design of a rather large rigid airship powered by "electro-magnetic circular power units" mounted on movable arms to control the direction of travel. The airship was never built.

May 30, 1899—Wilbur and Orville Wright requested information on heavier-than-air flight from the Smithsonian Institution. This letter was the first indication that the brothers had taken a serious interest in the problems of manned flight. The sons of a bishop of the United Brethren Church, the Wrights had demonstrated a normal youthful enthusiasm for flight. Presented with a toy helicopter, which they promptly broke, the brothers built larger models operating on the same principle. Ever eager to try new projects, they printed a successful neighborhood newspaper on a press they built. In response to the cycling craze which swept the nation in the 1890's, the Wrights set up a bicycle repair shop, where they eventually produced their own model. They maintained a casual interest in aeronautics throughout their adolescences, following the exploits of Otto Lilienthal in Germany, Samuel Pierpont Langley, Octave Chanute, and other experimenters. Reading about the death of Lilienthal in a gliding accident in 1896 seems to have been the impetus which led the Wrights to request information from the Smithsonian.

July 4, 1899—Leo Stevens, a Cleveland native, ascended unexpectedly when inexperienced members of his handling crew released his balloon prematurely. The craft rose rapidly, carrying several members of the ground crew who had become entangled in the ropes. Stevens was able to land safely in Lake Erie where all were rescued by passing fishermen. Stevens, who was frequently referred to as the nation's foremost aeronaut, made his first ascent in 1888 at the age of 15. He became a parachute jumper and balloon manufacturer, building one of the first successful powered airships in the nation in 1901. After he was appointed chief instructor for the U. S. Balloon Corps in 1907, he trained U. S. Army Signal Corps officers in the operation and handling of free and captive balloons.

September 1900—By this time (when Wilbur was 33 and Orville was 29 years old), the Wright brothers had completed their first glider and begun to search for a place where they could perform extensive test flights. Realizing that seclusion, soft soil, and constant winds were necessary, they chose the area close to Kill Devil Hill Life Saving Station near Kitty Hawk, N. C. This first Wright glider was a biplane employing the bridge truss system of wing support designed by Octave Chanute. It was flown as a kite, with the controls operated by ropes from the ground. The Wrights fixed on wing warping as the means of control. The operator on the ground pulled the correct control and the wing tip raised or dropped to bank the craft to the right or left.

July 1901—After building what they expected was an improved version of the glider, Wilbur and Orville Wright returned to Kitty Hawk. With this larger model they hoped to make manned glides. However, in spite of the increased area of the wings and control surfaces, the Wrights discovered that this glider was not as efficient as their 1900 model. Determined to discover the cause of failure, they returned to Dayton in August. In designing their gliders, the brothers had relied on the air pressure tables established by Lilienthal, Langley, and other engineers and scientists. Discovering that these tables were incorrect and that their inaccuracies were the primary cause of the failure of the 1901 machine, the Wrights constructed the first American wind tunnel and engaged in pioneer air pressure studies in an effort to determine the correct curvature for wings. These wind tunnel experiments provided the critical data which eventually insured that the Wright machine would be the first to fly.

September 1902—After rebuilding the glider, the brothers returned to Kitty Hawk. Although the 1902 glider proved more successful than earlier models, it demonstrated a tendency to nose into the ground when the wings were warped. The Wrights solved the problem by adding a single vertical rudder to the craft and connecting this to the wing warping system, so that when the wing tips moved up or down, the rudder moved to compensate and the airplane turned smoothly. Having developed a reliable system of control, the Wrights needed only to add power to the machine. Over 1000 successful flights were made prior to their return to Dayton in October 1902.

1903—Unable to find a light engine in their price range, the Wrights designed and constructed their own. They also developed propellers which proved to be more efficient than those previously designed. With the help of Charles Taylor, a bicycle mechanic, the brothers constructed the world's first successful powered airplane in Dayton during 1902-1903. By September 1903, Wilbur and Orville Wright were ready to depart for Kitty Hawk to test the craft. After reassembling the machine in a makeshift tent-hangar on the sand dunes, all was ready by December 14.

In front of the pilot was a stick which controlled the up and down motion of the craft. The pilot lay prone on the lower wing, and banked to the left or right by shifting his body in the proper direction in the cradle in which he lay. The 1903 *Flyer* was not equipped with wheels, but was launched on a wheeled cart which carried the craft down a single rail. To prevent the wings from touching the ground until the craft was airborne, a person ran alongside the *Flyer*.

Five volunteers from the Kill Devil Hill Life Saving Station were on hand—with a medical chest—as Wilbur, who had won the honor by lot, climbed onto the wing and eased himself into the cradle on December 14. The 12½ hp engine was revved and the catch which held the machine in check was released. The airplane raced down the track, left the earth at too sharp an angle, and fell in a stall.

December 17, 1903—Orville Wright made the world's first sustained, controlled, powered flight in history. Before the flight Orville set up his camera between the starting rail and the tent, focusing the lens on a point near the end of the rail. John T. Daniels, one of the men from the Life Saving Station who witnessed the flight, snapped the shutter seconds after the airplane left the track. The first flight lasted 12 seconds, during which the craft covered 120 feet. Three more flights were made on the 17th; the longest was 59 seconds, in which the machine traveled 852 feet. The Wrights were preparing to turn the *Flyer* around for a flight down the beach to the telegraph office at the Life Saving Station, when a sharp gust of wind overturned the machine, breaking the rudder spars, and effectively ending the 1903 flying season. Before leaving for Dayton, the brothers sent a telegram to their family, informing them of the success and the fact that they would be home for Christmas. Bishop Milton Wright notified the Dayton *Journal* of the contents of the historic message. The *Journal* dutifully informed its readers that the Wright boys, who had been vacationing in North Carolina, would be home for Christmas.

The Wright brothers with the airplane and hangar at Huffman Prairie, May 1904. Orville is standing at the wing tip on the left; Wilbur is on the right.

1904—The Wrights, having achieved successful powered flight, decided that their experiments could now be carried on closer to home. The first Ohio flights were made in a cow pasture owned by Torrence Huffman, a Dayton banker. The site was close to Simms Station near the Dayton-Fairborn interurban route, some eight miles from Dayton. Huffman refused payment for use of his field, asking only that the brothers put the animals pastured there outside the fence before attempting flights. Wilbur described the area as resembling a prairie dog town, because of the marshy surface and numerous chuckholes which were to plague the Wrights in the months to come. Also hazards were the trees and fences that bordered the area, which determined that long flights would be circles. The generally calm air which prevailed presented an additional handicap. Although flying would have been safer in calm air, experience had shown that it was almost impossible to get the airplane up in less than a 20 mile an hour head wind, which increased the airspeed. This problem was solved in September, when the Wrights erected a derrick and weight system which catapulted them into the air. The new arrangement permitted longer and more successful flights because the pilot was in complete control of the machine from the moment of takeoff. This solution overcame the mushy control which had plagued them when taking off at lower air speeds. Of the 105 flights made during the 1904 flying season, most were of extremely short duration. The first complete circle flown by an airplane, on September 20, was followed by other circuits of the field in December. The longest flight of 1904 lasted just over five minutes. Even though many technical problems remained to be solved, it was obvious that the Wright brothers were making real progress. The first published account of an airplane flight written by an eyewitness appeared in January 1905. A. I. Root, a Medina apiarist and publisher, visited the Wright flying field and published his impressions in his journal, *Gleanings in Bee Culture:*

> Dear friends, I have a wonderful story to tell you—a story that . . . outrivals the Arabian Nights fables—a story, too, with a moral that I think many of the younger ones need, and perhaps some of the older ones too. . . . I am now going to tell you of two . . . boys, a *minister's* boys, who love machinery, and who are interested in the modern developments of science and art. Their names are Orville and Wilbur Wright, of Dayton, Ohio. . . . These boys (they are men now), instead of spending their summer vacation with crowds, . . . went away by themselves to a desert place by the seacoast. . . . With a gliding machine made of sticks and cloth they learned to glide and soar from the top of a hill to the bottom; and by making . . . *more than a thousand* experiments, they became so proficient in guiding these gliding machines that they could sail like a bird, and control its movements up and down as well as sidewise. . . . At first there was considerable trouble about getting the machine up in the air and the engine well up to speed. . . . The machine is held until ready to start by a sort of trap to be sprung when all is ready; then with a tremendous flapping and snapping of the four-cylinder engine, the huge machine springs aloft. When it first turned that circle, and came near the starting-point, I was right in front of it; and I said then, and I believe still, it was one of the grandest sights, if not the grandest sight, of my life. Imagine a locomotive that has left its track, and is climbing up in the air right toward you—a locomotive without any wheels, we will say, but with white wings instead, we will *further* say—a locomotive made of aluminum. Well, now, imagine this white locomotive, with wings that spread 20 feet each way, coming right toward you with a tremendous flap of its propellers, and you will have something like what I saw. The younger brother bade me move to one side for fear it might come down suddenly; but I tell you, friends, the sensation which one feels in such a crisis is something hard to describe. . . . She [the airplane] made one of her very best flights . . . and as nobody else has as yet succeeded in doing any thing like what they have done I hope no millionaire or syndicate will try to rob them of the invention or laurels they have so fairly and honestly earned.

1904—A. Roy Knabenshue landed his airship *Toledo-1* on the roof of the ten story Spitzer building in Toledo. Knabenshue, a native of Bryan who had become interested in flight in 1900, had constructed a number of gliders which he flew from the stage of the old opera house in Bryan. Convinced that these craft were airworthy, Knabenshue shifted operations to a spot known locally as Beer Cellar Hill. He eventually discarded gliding and built a series of primitive dirigibles, the most successful of which was *Toledo-1*. Knabenshue subsequently came to national attention when he piloted Capt. Thomas Scott Baldwin's *California Arrow* in the St. Louis Air Meet. On August 20, 1905, he became the first man to fly over Manhattan, circling buildings to the delight of the crowds. A few years later, Knabenshue was employed by the Wright brothers to manage an exhibition team which toured the nation demonstrating the superiority of Wright machines. In this capacity he was able to hire such outstanding flyers as Ralph Johnstone, Arch Hoxsey, Phillip Parmalee, and Walter Brookins as charter members of the Wright team.

The start of the first flight of the 1905 flying season at Huffman Prairie, on June 23. The tower at the right served as the catapult launching device to get the airplane into the air in the light winds which prevailed in the area.

1905—Flights made from Huffman Prairie during 1905 demonstrated that most of the problems of control could be solved. The Wrights were able to ascend in their *Flyer* at will and remain aloft for relatively long periods of time, describing circles, figure-eights, and other patterns. Forty-nine flights were made between June 23 and October 16. The season was cut short by the appearances of large crowds to witness the flights. When the brothers had invited reporters to the first flights of 1904, they had not been able to get their machine into the air and the local papers had assumed that the Wrights were perpetrating a hoax. Obviously, it was ridiculous to expect two bicycle mechanics to accomplish what scientists and engineers could not! As reports of longer flights became common, however, the newspapers could no longer ignore them. The Wrights, who feared receiving extensive publicity prior to the grant of their patent, halted their experiments.

1905—Harry Christian Gammeter, a Cleveland inventor, began construction of two monoplanes, both of which proved to be unsuccessful.

September 7, 1905—Young Cromwell Dixon of Columbus was so impressed by a demonstration of a Knabenshue airship that he decided to construct his own. The boy visited Knabenshue in Toledo to receive instruction in the construction and operation of airships. In 1907 Dixon built his famous *Skycycle*, a small dirigible powered by bicycle pedals. Thirteen years old at the time, he was referred to as the "world's youngest aeronaut," and he received the congratulations of Knabenshue, Leo Stevens, the Wrights, and such European greats as Alberto Santos-Dumont and Henri Farman. The original *Skycycle*, which was destroyed in a fire, was replaced by a larger craft powered by a single cylinder Curtiss engine. In 1910, having become a featured performer on the aeronautical circuit, Dixon learned to fly an airplane and gave exhibitions throughout the nation.

September 6-7, 1906—Capt. Thomas Scott Baldwin, pioneer airship experimenter, exhibited his *California Arrow* in Dayton and Columbus. Similar to the smaller dirigibles which were flown at county fairs across the state, Baldwin's craft employed a lightweight motorcycle engine constructed by Glenn H. Curtiss, a young motorcycle racer from Hammondsport, N. Y. When engine trouble plagued Capt. Baldwin during his Ohio trip, Curtiss paid his first visit to the state to repair the motor, which allowed the aeronaut to continue his tour.

September 30, 1906—The first James Gordon Bennett Trophy was awarded to Lt. Frank Purdy Lahm and Maj. H. B. Hersey. In their balloon *United States*, Lahm, a native of Mansfield, and Hersey traveled from Paris to Whitby, Yorkshire, England—a distance of 410 miles in 22 hours and 17 minutes.

September 2, 1907—Walter Wellman of Lake County attempted to fly to the North Pole in his semirigid dirigible, *America*. The founder of the Cincinnati *Penny Paper*, which later became the *Post and Times-Star*, Wellman had a lifelong interest in polar exploration. During the winters of 1898 and 1899 he had attempted to reach the pole by sledge, but had achieved only a latitude of 82° north. Concluding that the airship offered the only practical means of conquering the polar ice pack, he ordered the *America* from a French firm. Like most explorers of the period, Wellman chose Spitsbergen, Norway, as his starting point. The trip was cut short by a violent storm encountered after only a few hours of travel.

1908—The Roberts Motor Company, producers of fine marine engines, moved to Sandusky. Recognizing the need for lightweight reliable engines to power the frail aircraft of the period, the Roberts company became one of the first American firms to enter the field.

January 28, 1908—Frank Lahm, Henry Alden, and J. G. Obermier made a balloon flight from Canton, Ohio, to Oil City, Pa., a distance of 100 miles, in two hours.

1908—Charles Stroble, a Sandusky promoter, built a series of airships in Toledo. He employed a number of prominent figures to demonstrate his machines, including Lincoln Beachey and Cleveland-born Stanley Vaughn.

August 8, 1908—Wilbur Wright made his first successful European flight at Le Mans, France. Although the Brazilian-born Santos-Dumont had previously flown in his *14-bis* and other experimenters had left the ground for short hops, no other aircraft could compare with the Wright machine in performance. These spectacular French flights proved to the world that the Wrights were not "bluffeurs" as had been supposed. The nearly five years' time between the first successful flight and the official unveiling of the craft in Europe had enabled the brothers to accomplish truly sustained controlled flight.

September 9, 1908—Lt. Frank Lahm went aloft with Orville Wright during the Army trials of the Wright machine at Ft. Myer, Va. Lahm thus became the first Army officer to make an official flight in an airplane.

September 17, 1908—Orville Wright, flying with Lt. Thomas Selfridge, a member of Dr. Alexander Graham Bell's Aerial Experiment Association, crashed the Wright *Flyer* at Ft. Myer. Orville escaped with a broken leg and minor injuries, but Selfridge died. Army officials were so impressed with the performance of the machine despite the accident, that an extension was granted so that trials might continue after Orville's recovery.

1909—Matthew B. Sellers of Norwood, Ohio, constructed a successful quadruplane powered by a seven hp engine. Although the machine set no records, it did fly.

June 17-18, 1909—Wilbur and Orville Wright received gold medals from Pres. William Howard Taft, Gov. Judson B. Harmon, and the mayor of Dayton, Edward E. Burkhardt.

Following their return to Dayton, the Wright brothers continued to use Huffman Prairie as a flying field and established the nation's first flying school on the site. The following list of students who soloed at the field contains the names of many who were to make aviation history: Henry H. (Hap) Arnold, who commanded the Army Air Force during World War II and served as the first Air Force chief of staff; Lt. Frank Lahm, an early leader in the fight for a stronger American air arm; Lt. John Rodgers and Lt. Kenneth Whiting, the nation's first naval aviators; Lt. Charles DeForest Chandler, an early Army aviator; Calbraith P. Rodgers, the first man to fly from coast to coast; Capt. Roy A. Brown, a Canadian pilot often credited with the death of the great World War I German ace Manfred von Richthofen; Walter Brookins, Phillip Parmalee, Ralph Johnstone, Arch

Hoxsey, and Duval LaChapelle, all of whom were to become instructors at the Wright school or members of the Wright exhibition team which toured the nation publicizing Wright airplanes. Others who soloed at Huffman Prairie included: Lt. Thomas Milling, Griffith Brewer, B. Fowler, A. Welsh, Frank Coffyn, J. C. Turpin, Howard Gill, L.W. Bonney, O. A. Brindley, J. C. Henning, Harold Brown, R. J. Arnor, Harry Atwood, H. V. Hills, Louie Mitchell, O. G. Simmons, C. Couterier, Wilfred Stevens, Arch Freeman, J. G. Klocker, Farnum Priest, C. Webster, Al Elton, Andrew Drew, O. A. Merrill, Phil Page, G. Gray, John Bixler, B. Whelan, Howard Rinehart, A. Bressman, M. T. Shemerhorm, R. M. Wright, W. Bowersox, L. E. Brown, A. B. Gaines, C. Peterson, L. Norman, C. Utter, C. Terrell, Mrs. Richberg Hornsby, C. Day, Mary Stinson, C. Ando, Frank Kitamura, O. A. Danielson, Lyle Scott, Fred Eggena, R. E. Lee, Rose Dugan, M. Alexander, J. McRae, Garoku Moro, Vern Carter, E. P. Beckwith, T. Pemberton, B. Lewis, Maurice Coombs, George Simpson, Gordon Ross, K. Macdonald, Percy Beasely, H. Saunders, M. Galbraith, W. J. Sussan, C. J. Kreery, John P. Galpin, Floyd Breadner, C. Nudig, A. Briggs, H. Evans, Basil Hobbs, James Gordon, Ed Stinson, M. Dubuc, J. Shaw, A. Harland, H. Smith, W. Chiam, Robert Weir, G. Magar, N. Magar, J. Bibbey, G. Harrower, J. C. Walston, S. T. Edwards, Harry Swan, A. G. Woodward, L. Ault, A. Wilks, J. Simpson, Paul Godbois, G. McNicoll, W. E. Robinson, M. Beal, C. Bronson, W. Orchard, J. Harmon, T. Wilkinson, J. G. Ireland, Fred Southard, Grover Bergdoll, Charles Wald, and Will Kabitzke.

July 22, 1909—Arthur Holly Compton, native of Wooster who was to win the Nobel prize for physics in 1927, launched a homemade glider from a hill near his Wayne County home. On this initial flight the craft was weighted with sandbags to gauge its stability in the air. On the morning of April 3, 1910, the 17-year-old Compton himself made a number of flights, the longest 185 feet. The youth's early interest in aeronautics had led previously to his first published scientific article, "Comparison of Wright and Voisin Aeroplanes," in *Scientific American*, February 1909.

1909—Stanley Vaughn, an airship pilot employed by Charles Stroble, performed all over Ohio during the summers of 1909 and 1910. His tours included Xenia, Cincinnati, Findlay, Bryan, and Niles. His airship was 56 feet long, powered by an Indian motorcycle engine. The aeronaut stood on a catwalk beneath the gasbag. In order to bring the nose of the ship down, he walked to the front; to climb, he walked to the rear.

August 2, 1909—The U. S. government purchased its first airplane from the Wright brothers for $30,000. Until 1911 this was the only airplane owned by the government. Lt. B. D. Foulois, the only Army officer on flying duty, who was responsible for the machine and its maintenance, often paid for repairs out of his own pocket. Lt. Foulois, who was not a trained pilot, learned to fly the machine by trial and error and through extensive correspondence with the Wrights.

Preparing the Wright airplane for the successful Army trials of 1909.

August 15, 1909—Walter Wellman attempted a second polar crossing in his airship, *America*. Following the failure of this attempt and the successful overland journey of Adm. Robert E. Peary, Wellman abandoned his Arctic explorations as he had "no desire to play second fiddle in discovery."

January 1910—The Cleveland Aero Club, whose members specialized in the construction of heavier-than-air machines, was founded.

June 28, 1910—Capt. William Mattery circled the Cleveland Country Club twice at an altitude of five to ten feet to give residents of that city their first look at an airplane in flight.

July 24, 1910—Harry Ginter of Cleveland built an airship similar to those of Knabenshue and Thomas Baldwin. After several unsuccessful attempts he succeeded in flying from Luna Park to Cedar Avenue and back.

August 28, 1910—R. J. Linley crashed a biplane constructed by C. W. Caine in Cleveland's Luna Park. Linley, who had never soloed, panicked as the plane left the ground; he dived over the side and allowed the machine to smash into a fence.

August 29, 1910—Earl Wiseman of Cleveland lifted his home-built monoplane to an altitude of three feet for a 100 yard flight.

Orville Wright aloft over Dayton in a Wright airplane, September 1910. Note the balloon inflation on Buck Island.

August 31, 1910—Glenn Hammond Curtiss flew from Euclid Beach, Cleveland, to Cedar Point, returning to Cleveland by air the next day. The management of Euclid Beach awarded the aviator a $5000 prize for this record-breaking over-water flight which covered more than 60 miles. Curtiss flew his already famous *Hudson Flyer*, powered by an eight cylinder, 50 hp engine, in which he had earlier flown down the Hudson River from Albany to New York.

October 12-15, 1910—The Cleveland Air Meet was held in Lakeview Park. Directed by Glenn Curtiss, the meet featured a number of famous flyers, including Augustus Post, J. A. D. Macurdy, J. C. "Bud" Mars, and Eugene Ely, the first man to take off and land on an American ship at sea.

October 13, 1910—Cleveland aviator Harvey Harkness, who had hoped to win the Harvard Aviation Trophy at a New York air meet, was unable to compete because he crashed his machine at a Boston meet.

October 15, 1910—Walter Wellman attempted to cross the Atlantic in the *America*. Although the flight was cut short by strong winds and engine problems which forced a landing in the ocean, it did set world records for speed and distance covered in an airship. Also, for the first time in history, messages were sent from land to an airship over the water.

A Wright Model B machine under construction in the Wright factory in Dayton, 1910 or 1911.

November 7, 1910—Phillip Parmalee, a member of the Wright exhibition team, flew the world's first air freight shipment. Bolts of silk were tied to his machine in Dayton for the flight to Columbus, where the silk was distributed to spectators.

1910—Walter Brookins, also of the Wright exhibition team, made the first night flight in history, in Alabama. Brookins, a native of Dayton, also was the first pilot to demonstrate aerobatics over Indianapolis, where he won a $5000 prize for establishing a new altitude mark of 6175 feet. He was one of the few individuals who received personal flying instruction from the Wrights.

Glenn Curtis takes off for his flight to Cedar Point on August 31, 1910.

1911—Reinhardt Ausmus of Sandusky built a Bleriot type monoplane.

April 29, 1911—Earl Wiseman of Cleveland announced the forthcoming production and sales of his design of airplanes.

May 6, 1911—The Dyeoplane Company of Newport and the Clark Airship Company of Cleveland were incorporated.

May 1911—Charles Stroble of Toledo prepared his exhibition team for appearances at county fairs. Among the group was 17-year-old Howard LeVan, who had previously made a flight from Bay View Park, Cleveland, to Toledo and back.

May 29-June 3, 1911—Phillip Parmalee, Earl Ovington, Tom Sopwith, and Capt. Thomas Baldwin participated in the Columbus Air Meet. Parmalee, flying a Wright machine, sent messages to a ground station. Races were held, including a slow flying event won by Parmalee who flew two seconds slower than Sopwith. A chalk bomb-dropping contest and aerobatics were included in the program.

June 15, 1911—Glenn Curtiss returned to Cleveland to demonstrate his new hydroplane.

July 7, 1911—John Gammeter made a number of exhibition flights at Silver Lake, Akron.

July 8, 1911—Calbraith Perry Rodgers crashed a Wright plane at the Dayton Country Club.

July 11, 1911—Edward and Milton Korn of Shelby County flew one of the first successful pusher monoplanes in the nation.

August 1911—Harry Atwood, a pioneer stunt pilot, performed in Sandusky. This city, which was already the home of the Roberts Motor Company, was to become a major aviation center in the years before World War I.

September 3-5, 1911—Albert Elton and A. L. Welsh set a distance record for flight with a passenger as they flew from Dayton to Youngstown. The pair covered 244 miles, with stops in Columbus, Pickerington, Newark, Wakatomika, Trinway, and Salem, Ohio.

September 4, 1911—The Curzon Aviators performed at Mt. Vernon.

September 1911—Blanche Scott made a number of appearances in the state. Miss Scott, an actress, was one of the nation's first women pilots. She later won stellar roles in such productions as *An Aviator and an Automobilist Race for a Bride.*

September 14, 1911—Mr. Mora, "a new aviator," was slightly injured when his machine fell 50 feet to earth during an Akron flight.

September 22, 1911—Frank Miller died in a Dayton crash. His gasoline tank exploded in flight, sending the airplane to the earth in flames.

September 28, 1911—Canton hosted an air meet. Pilots attending the meet included Harry Atwood, who crashed his Demoiselle machine; Eugene Ely, Walter Brookins, Arthur Stone, Rene Simon, Ladis Lawkowicz, and Andrew Drew, who crashed his Curtiss machine into a fence near the spectators.

September 30, 1911—Cromwell Dixon of Columbus, now recognized as one of the nation's foremost aeronauts, won a $10,000 prize as the first man to fly the main range of the Rocky Mountains. On October 2, 1911, Dixon was killed in a crash at Spokane, Wash.

November 4, 1911—The first flight of the airship *Akron* was made. Melvin Vanniman, who had served as navigator on Walter Wellman's *America* crew, hoped to be able to make a transatlantic flight in the 400,000 cubic foot dirigible constructed by the Goodyear Tire and Rubber Company of Akron. However, the airship and crew were lost when the balloon exploded on a trial flight near Atlantic City, N. J.

November 11, 1911—C. P. Wanzer of Urbana, a pilot and aircraft manufacturer, applied for an airmail contract. The Post Office Department, unwilling to risk the mail in an airplane, rejected the application.

1912—The Akron Aviation Company and the Dayton Paraoplane Company were founded.

January 1912—The Rider brothers of Newark purchased an airplane and planned an exhibition tour through the South.

May 21, 1912—Fred Southard stole an airplane at the Wright flying field near Dayton and went aloft for his solo flight. Southard fell 100 feet to his death when the engine failed.

May 30, 1912—Wilbur Wright died in Dayton of typhoid fever.

This series of photos, taken during a flight at Bryan, Ohio, on July 4, 1911, illustrates the launching, flight, and crash of an early exhibition airship piloted by Stanley I. Vaughn.

Stanley Vaughn Collection

33

Edward Korn with the Korn brothers' Benoist, in which Edward made several exhibition flights at Botkins, Shelby County, May 30, 1912. The picture clearly shows the elevator, rudder, and ailerons, all flexing surfaces.

Summer 1912—The Curtiss exhibition team entertained Ohioans at the Portsmouth Air Meet on May 31-June 1; the Lima Air Show, June 6-8; the Mansfield Air Show, June 7-9, and the Springfield Air Meet, July 30-August 3.

June 1, 1912—Phillip Parmalee, a member of the original Wright exhibition team, died in a crash at Yakima, Wash.

June 5, 1912—Col. C. B. Winder of the Ohio National Guard became the nation's first National Guard pilot.

June 20, 1912—Edward Korn and C. Ray Benedict gave an exhibition in Youngstown.

July 12-13, 1912—Lincoln Beachey and Beckworth Havens demonstrated their machines in Hamilton.

July 20, 1912—George Schmitt made exhibition flights in Alliance and East Liverpool on the same day.

July 27, 1912—Charles W. Saunders made a series of parachute jumps from F. W. Kemper's Wright plane at Silver Lake, Akron.

August 20, 1912—Cecil Paoli reached an altitude of 3200 feet while flying at Findlay.

August 21, 1912—George Smith flew 25 miles from Bellefontaine to Kenton.

August 23-24, 1912—Paul Peck gave a successful exhibition in Marion.

August 29, 1912—Paul Peck demonstrated his skill to the citizens of Massillon. Peck died in the crash of his Columbia biplane in Chicago on September 11, 1912.

September 14, 1912—While flying at a carnival in Leetonia, Ohio, John St. Clair fell from his machine. He suffered only minor injuries because his fall was "broken somewhat" when he hit power lines.

October 6, 1912—Earl Sandt escaped serious injury when he hit a railing during a landing at Lorain.

December 12, 1912—The Weldon B. Cooke Aeroplane Company was incorporated at Sandusky.

1913—A Goodyear balloon won the James Gordon Bennett Trophy balloon race.

January 13, 1913—J. C. Barbazon and Frank Shuffer established a flying school in Lima.

January 1913—The Cincinnati Aero Club was founded.

April 1913—Bert W. Bean of Celina built a series of "land planes and hydroplanes."

April 30, 1913—Weldon Cooke's hydroplane *Irene*, capable of 35 mph on the water and 50 mph in the air, raced C. B. Lockwood's speedboat *Chinook*.

Summer 1913—Weldon Cooke and Harry Atwood planned a passenger service between Sandusky, Cedar Point, and Put-in-Bay. The fare from Sandusky to Cedar Point was to be $10 with an additional $25 for the trip to the island.

May 5, 1913—Charles Carson of Milwaukee was killed when his plane crashed at Silver Lake, Akron.

May 10, 1913—Andrew Drew made a series of 25 flights over Lima.

May 27, 1913—Harry Atwood was forced down on Lake Erie in a flying boat. Atwood remained afloat on the lake for four hours before rescue, inadvertently demonstrating the seaworthiness of his craft.

Edward Korn flying a 1913 Benoist tractor biplane. The picture was taken in flight by a camera fastened to a wing strut. The Roberts motor, built in Sandusky, could fly up to 65 mph.

June 1913—Andrew Drew made a flight over Springfield, then went on to Lima, where he was killed on June 12 when his airplane exploded at an altitude of 200 feet.

June 1913—Edward Korn flew from Montra to Botkins for an exhibition before an exceptionally large crowd.

June 28, 1913—Paul Studenski, in a National biplane, performed with the Curtiss aviators at Silver Lake, Akron.

July 1913—Al Engel demonstrated his "aerohydroplane" to the citizens of Cleveland.

July 1913—Harry Atwood enjoyed a record month for passengers from Toledo.

July 17-20, 1913—Katherine Stinson, one of America's foremost women pilots, flew at Coney Island, Cincinnati.

July 26, 1913—Atwood performed spirals over Lorain from an altitude of 3000 feet.

July 28, 1913—Al Engel thrilled the citizens of Ashtabula with an exhibition given in his Curtiss machine.

August 1913—Edward Korn opened a flying school at Jackson Center and continued to exhibit his machine all over the state. On August 13, 1913, while flying with his brother Milton near their home in Montra, Shelby County, Korn crashed his Benoist tractor biplane. Although the pilot survived, Milton Korn died in the crash.

August 1913—E. Holt flew in Akron.

August 14, 1913—Harry Atwood and Beckworth Havens flew 71 miles on a trip from Toledo to Detroit in 65 minutes.

September 1913—H. P. Harris flew over Cuyahoga Falls and Monroe Falls. On September 19 Harris moved to Akron, where he made a series of flights, one of which lasted 51 minutes.

September 1913—Harry Atwood demonstrated the advantages of his hydroplane to a group of National Guard and Naval Reserve officers meeting in Sandusky.

September 27, 1913—Weldon B. Cooke escaped serious injury as his plane's wheels dug into the mud and overturned the aircraft in a landing at Canton. Cooke previously that day had completed a flight to Massillon and back.

November 1913—Weldon Cooke was employed by the Akron *Press* to drop copies of that paper over the city.

November 1913—Paul Wilbur circled New London for half an hour in his Curtiss type machine.

November 1913—A. Roy Knabenshue constructed the nation's first passenger carrying dirigible in Pasadena, Calif.

December 1913—Orville Wright conducted flight tests on the new Wright Model G, a flying boat. He remained an active pilot throughout this period.

December 1913—An aeroboat show was held in Toledo.

December 13, 1913—Ohio-born ambassador to France, Myron T. Herrick, made his first flight in an airplane, going aloft with the famous French stunt pilot Alphonse Pegoud. Herrick was to become one of aviation's most enthusiastic boosters during the period following World War I.

December 13, 1913—Orville Wright was awarded the Collier Trophy, honoring the most important contribution to the science of aeronautics made in that year, for his development of an automatic stabilizer.

May 9, 1914—Tom W. Benoist announced that his St. Louis-based company, Benoist Aircraft, would move to Sandusky, Ohio. Benoist was one of the leaders of the nation's youthful aviation industry.

June 4, 1914—A. C. Beech smashed his Gyro machine at Zanesville.

Summer 1914—Anthony Jannus established a flying boat service at Sandusky. In January 1914, Jannus, in a Benoist flying boat, had inaugurated the nation's first regularly scheduled airline flights as he carried passengers and freight across Tampa Bay, Fla.

August 1914—Lincoln Beachey, who had become one of the nation's most famous aviators since his days as a stunt pilot for Charles Stroble in Sandusky, returned to Ohio to give a series of exhibition flights. The first American to loop an airplane, Beachey presented his usual "looping and upside down flying" during this tour of the state. He appeared before capacity crowds in Dayton, Toledo, Lima, New Lexington, Cincinnati, and Cleveland. During his appearance at the North Randall Race Track near Cleveland, the intrepid birdman thrilled the crowds by racing the famous Barney Oldfield around the track. Beachey was killed on March 14, 1915, while performing for the Panama-Pacific Exposition in San Francisco.

September 14, 1914—Weldon B. Cooke died in a plane crash at Pueblo, Colo. His plane fell to earth during a turn past the reviewing stand where Gov. Elias M. Ammons and his staff were assembled.

September 20, 1914—Art Smith, flying at Toledo, climbed to 1800 feet, performed seven consecutive loops as he descended to 300 feet, and rolled his Curtiss machine eight times.

October 1, 1914—Earl Dougherty escaped serious injury when he crashed his Beachey tractor biplane near Eaton.

1917—The C-1, the first Goodyear naval airship, was delivered. Ohioan Stanley Vaughn, as a representative of the Curtiss company, was involved in the design of the ship's control car.

April 9, 1917—An era in aviation history began with the formation of the Dayton-Wright Airplane Company. Organized by Edward A. Deeds, Charles F. Kettering, H. E. Talbott, and H. E. Talbott, Jr., the company's original purpose was to undertake aeronautical research and development, rather than production of aircraft. Orville Wright served as consulting engineer. In August 1917, however, the group received an order for 500 training machines and 5000 Liberty engine DH-4 airplanes. South Field, the company's experimental flying field near Dayton, became the site for many important aeronautical developments during World War I. It was here, for example, that Dr. Frank K. Jewett, chief engineer for the Western Electric Company, perfected air-to-air radio transmission. In 1918 the Dayton-Wright Company produced 3506 airplanes.

April 1917—Howard Coffin, a native of West Milton, Ohio, and a former vice president of the Hudson Motor Car Company, was appointed chairman of the newly-created Aircraft Production Board. The board's primary responsibility was to choose aircraft types to be produced by American firms and to insure that the finished airplanes were delivered in sufficient quantities to the Army and Navy.

May 17, 1917—Edward A. Deeds was appointed to the Aircraft Production Board. He served until August 2, 1917, when he was inducted into the Army with the rank of colonel and became acting chief of the Equipment Division of the Army Air Service. In this capacity Deeds was responsible for one of the most important American contributions to the war effort— the development of the Liberty engine. Deeds, aware that the number of different engine types manufactured by the allied powers created enormous problems of supply and maintenance at the front, was determined to provide one standard "all American" engine to power American aircraft. He presented the problem to J. G. Vincent of the Packard Company and E. J. Hall of the Hall-Scott Company. Within 48 hours of their first meeting, the rough design for the Liberty engine was complete. Less than six weeks after the completion of the design, the Packard Company had produced the first eight cylinder model, rated at 220 hp. A 12 cylinder model, which eventually achieved 440 hp, was also produced. By May 29, 1918, one year after the meeting between Deeds, Hall, and Vincent, 1100 Liberty engines had been produced. The ignition system for the engine was designed by Charles F. Kettering of Dayton. The Liberty engine continued in use for some years after the war, powering many of the early postwar Air Service record-breaking aircraft, as well as the NC-4's, the first airplanes to fly the Atlantic, and the Douglas World Cruisers, the first planes to circumnavigate the globe.

May 25, 1917—Capt. J. C. Waring of the U. S. Army Signal Corps Construction Division arrived at a site near Fairfield (now part of Fairborn), which had been chosen for establishment of Wilbur Wright Field, an Army Air Service training center. On June 6 Capt. A. R. Christie arrived to take command of the site. Flying cadets received an eight week course in theoretical aeronautics at The Ohio State University before reporting to Wilbur Wright Field for basic flight instruction. Advanced training in combat flying and aerobatics was given after the students arrived in France. On June 16, 1917, the Signal Corps established the Fairfield Air Depot, a supply center, on a 40 acre tract adjacent to the flying field. This area eventually became part of the Wright-Patterson Air Force Base complex.

June 14, 1917—Tom W. Benoist was killed as he struck a telephone pole while leaning from a streetcar.

June 19, 1917—Adm. Robert E. Peary, discoverer of the North Pole, visited Sandusky to inspect the Benoist company, naval contractors.

1917—"The Bug," a pilotless bomb, was developed by Charles F. Kettering, Orville Wright, William Chryst, Thomas Midgley, and John Sheats at the Dayton-Wright Company's South Field. The "Bug," a small biplane built of wood, had a 15 foot wingspan and gyroscopic flight controls. The device contained a mechanism for measuring the distance flown; at a predetermined point, the craft's wings fell off and the fuselage, carrying a 100 pound charge of TNT, fell to earth. The "Bug" proved so successful in its trial flights that the government ordered 20,000 and trained students of Massachusetts Institute of Technology to service and launch them. However, the armistice was signed before any "Bugs" could be shipped to France.

August 1917—The Engle Aircraft Company of Niles, Ohio, was organized, with George Patterson as president and Al Engle, a pioneer Curtiss pilot, as vice president and production manager. By the fall of 1917 the company was producing JN-4D training planes for the Air Service.

October 17, 1917—McCook Field was established at Dayton as the nation's first Air Service engineering test center. Named for the "Fighting McCooks" of Civil War fame, who had originally owned the land on which the field was constructed, McCook soon became the major center in the nation for progress in American military and civilian aeronautics.

October 29, 1917—The first American built DH-4 was flown in Dayton. Soon after America's entry into World War I, U. S. Air Service officials discovered that in nearly three years of combat experience in the skies over France, the airplane had become a formidable weapon of war. Rather than attempt the development of distinct American types of warplanes, American firms were instructed to contract with European manufacturers to produce proven designs already in service with allied air forces. The DH-4, a British two seat observation and bombing machine, was the first of these types selected for American manufacture. The classic American basic trainer of the period, the JN-4 Jenny, was designed by Cleveland native Stanley I. Vaughn for the Curtiss company of Hammondsport, N. Y. As engineer and factory manager for the company, Vaughn was involved in the production of virtually all the planes produced by Curtiss.

February 1918—The Glenn L. Martin Company opened a new plant at 16800 St. Clair Ave., Cleveland. With Lawrence Bell as factory manager and Donald W. Douglas as chief engineer, the factory produced the famous Martin bomber, the MB-1, the first large military bomber purchased by the Army Air Service. Although the MB-1 appeared too late for service in France, it became the backbone of the American bombing fleet in the years immediately following the war. In 1921 Gen. William Mitchell employed Martin bombers to destroy the "unsinkable" German dreadnought *Ostfriesland* during bombing trials held off Hampton Roads, Va.

May 15, 1918—Airmail service was established between Chicago and Cleveland.

September 25, 1918—Lt. Edward V. Rickenbacker, of the American 94th Aero Squadron, attacked seven enemy aircraft near Billy, France. A native of Columbus, Rickenbacker was an automobile mechanic and race driver prior to shipping to France, where he served as Gen. John J. Pershing's chauffeur. A chance meeting with Gen. William Mitchell, who was then commanding Air Service tactical units of the AEF, led to Rickenbacker's appointment as a flying cadet. He served his apprenticeship as a combat airman under Maj. Raoul Lufberry, a veteran of the French Lafayette Flying Corps, and eventually rose to command of the 94th. Rickenbacker ended the war as the American Ace of Aces, with a score of 26 victories. Following the war he served as president of Eastern Airlines and during World War II made a series of personal inspections of frontline combat areas.

Ohio's second ranking ace was First Lt. Harvey Cook of Toledo, who was awarded the Distinguished Service Cross. Like Rickenbacker, Cook was a member of the famed 94th Aero Squadron, known as the "Hat-in-the-Ring" squadron because of their insigne, which symbolized America's entrance into the war. He downed seven enemy aircraft.

Lt. David Ingalls of Cleveland was the nation's only naval ace of the First World War. Ingalls, attached to the 213th Squadron of the Royal Air Force, destroyed five German machines. He was awarded the Distinguished Service Medal and the Distinguished Service Cross. Active in Ohio politics following the war, he was instrumental in the passage of the state's first aeronautical regulatory legislation. Ingalls returned to naval aviation during World War II, serving as chief of staff for Air Center Control Forward Area on Guadalcanal. He was awarded the Bronze Star for his work in the Pacific and retired as a rear admiral in the Naval Reserve.

Lt. Frederick E. Cook of Cleveland downed five enemy aircraft while serving with the U. S. 25th Aero Squadron, after having transferred from the RAF 74th Squadron. Lt. Robert M. Todd, a native of Cincinnati, claimed five victories while serving with the 17th Aero Squadron.

In addition to those Ohioans who served with American units, a number distinguished themselves in the French Air Service. Robert L. Rockwell of Cincinnati served as adjutant with Nieuport 124, the famous Lafayette Escadrille, prior to transfer to the American 103rd Pursuit Squadron. Cincinnatian Stephen Hinkle was a sergeant pilot in the Escadrille until he was discharged when it was discovered that he was overage. Charles H. Veil of East Palestine, Ohio, flew with Spad 150, transferring to the U. S. Air Service at America's entry into the war.

1919—The J. V. Martin Company of Elyria developed a seven ton, twin engine bomber.

1919—Elwood "Sam" Junkin, Clayton Bruckner, Charles Meyers, "Buck" Weaver, and E. P. Lott founded the Weaver Aircraft Company in Lorain, Ohio. WACO's numbers 1, 2, and 3, small aircraft with lightweight engines, were unsuccessful. Following the departure of Weaver and Meyers, the company was reorganized as Advanced Aircraft and produced biplanes with Curtiss OX-5 engines. WACO migrated to Alliance and then Medina and finally settled in Troy, where the WACO 6 was produced. Following this difficult period, the company entered an era of growth, producing some of the most popular private airplanes to appear in the 1920's and 1930's.

April 28, 1919—Leslie Irving of the McCook Field staff made the first jump with a backpack, free type parachute. The development of such a device was a major objective of Air Service officials in the years after World War I.

May 16, 1919—The Navy's NC-4, a Curtiss flying boat, completed the first air crossing of the Atlantic. One of the plane's pilots was Lt. Walter Hinton of Van Wert. In 1922 Hinton flew the *Friendship Flight* on the first flight from New York to Rio de Janeiro.

May 1919—The Goodyear blimp A4 moored on the roof of Cleveland's Statler Hotel.

July 1919—Airmail and freight service was inaugurated between Cleveland and New York.

October 30, 1919—Engineers at McCook Field tested the first reversible pitch propeller.

February 27, 1920—Maj. Rudolph Schroeder set an official altitude mark of 33,113 feet in a LePere biplane with a Liberty engine at McCook. Dressed in warm flying clothes, Schroeder planned to use two oxygen systems to enable him to climb above 30,000 feet. Hoping to conduct a number of experiments in the upper atmosphere, he was especially anxious to investigate the high speed winds said to exist above 25,000 feet. However, the automatic oxygen system which he had expected to employ at high altitude failed, forcing him to rely on a small flask which fed oxygen through a metal stem held in the pilot's mouth. When this flask emptied at 33,000 feet and Schroeder was unable to attach another cylinder to the mechanism, he pushed the nose of the plane into a dive. Lapsing into unconsciousness, he fell to 3000 feet before regaining his senses and pulling out of the dive for a landing. Schroeder continued his experimental work until his retirement from the Air Service in 1921. He was later named superintendent of the airline which the Ford Motor Company operated between Detroit, Chicago, and Cleveland.

May 4, 1920—Capt. L. I. Snow of McCook Field was forced to land a German Fokker D-7 powered by a Liberty engine in the waters of the Miami River. Snow was taking part in a series of tests to determine the airworthiness of airframes produced by other nations during World War I. Realizing that the airplane would remain afloat, he calmly perched on the tail and awaited rescuers.

May 6, 1920—Lt. Meister of the McCook Field engineering section crashed and burned a French Nieuport following an engine failure in flight. Rescuers rushed to the scene expecting to find the pilot seriously injured, but were happily surprised to find him crawling on the ground in search of a pair of goggles thrown overboard prior to the crash.

October 31, 1920—Planes carrying Socialist campaign literature for Eugene V. Debs "bombed" Toledo.

January 24, 1921—Myron T. Herrick of Cleveland was elected president of the Aero Club of America.

August 4, 1921—Five thousand catalpa trees near Troy were sprayed from an airplane in one of the earliest recorded instances in which the airplane was used to dust crops.

The Cleveland-built Martin MB-1 bomber, the nation's first heavy bombing type. The plane gained particular fame as the craft employed by Assistant Chief of the Air Service William Mitchell during bombing trials off Hampton Roads, Va., in 1921.

September 28, 1921—Lt. John A. Macready reached a record altitude of 34,508 feet over McCook Field in a supercharged LePere biplane.

April 6, 1922—Lt. Macready took the LePere to 34,563 feet.

June 12, 1922—Lt. Albert W. Stevens made a parachute jump from a record altitude of 24,200 feet over McCook Field.

July 1922—Lt. Donald Bruner of the McCook Field staff conducted extensive night flying tests leading to the development of landing lights and safety equipment.

July 14, 1922—Aeromarine Airways opened Cleveland to Detroit service.

August 15, 1922—A Ford was delivered to a Cleveland automobile dealer by the Aeromarine flying boat *Buckeye*.

August 16, 1922—The Sperry airway light was tested at McCook Field.

October 20, 1922—Lt. H. R. Harris had to jump from his airplane at an altitude of 2500 feet when the engine failed. This was one of the first occasions in which an American pilot's life was saved by a parachute.

December 18, 1922—Maj. F. H. Bane successfully flew the DeBothezat helicopter for 1 minute and 42 seconds. This machine, which was constructed at McCook Field, was one of the first vertical lift craft to enjoy even limited success.

Maj. Rudolph Schroeder, a McCook Field test pilot, stands beside his Vervile-Packard racer.

U. S. Air Force Museum

January 5, 1923—Prof. W. D. Bancroft of Cornell University accomplished the first successful cloud seeding from an Air Service machine over McCook Field.

March 29, 1923—Lts. H. R. Harris and Ralph Lockwood set a new world speed record of 125.42 miles per hour as they flew a DH-4L 400 at Wilbur Wright Field. That same day Lt. Russell L. Maughan set a world speed record of 236.587 miles per hour in the Curtiss 465 racer.

March 31, 1923—Lt. Alexander Pearson set a world speed record in the Vervile-Sperry racer as he flew the 500 kilometer course at Dayton.

April 16-17, 1923—Lts. John Macready and Oakley G. Kelly established endurance and distance records as they flew their Fokker T-2 monoplane over a triangular course at Wilbur Wright Field for 36 hours, 4 minutes, and 32 seconds. The pair also set speed records for the 2500, 3500, and 4000 kilometer courses.

April 17, 1923—Lt. H. R. Harris set a world speed record for the 1500 kilometer course in a DH-4 Liberty 375.

May 2-3, 1923—Lts. Kelly and Macready made the first nonstop transcontinental flight in the Fokker T-2. Departing from Roosevelt Field on New York's Long Island, they landed at Rockwell Field, San Diego, after a flight of 26 hours and 50 minutes. Upon their return to McCook on May 8, the pilots of the Engineering Division gave an "aerial circus" in their honor.

June 20, 1923—The CO-1, the first all metal aircraft acquired by the Air Service, was test flown. McCook Field engineers had designed and supervised the construction of the aircraft.

The Barling Bomber, NBL-1, on its first test flight from Wilbur Wright Field on August 22, 1923. The pilots, Lt. H. R. Harris and Lt. M. S. Fairchild, were accompanied by a mechanic and the plane's designer, Walter Barling.

August 22, 1923—The Barling Bomber, the world's largest airplane, was successfully test flown at Wilbur Wright Field by Lt. H. R. Harris. On October 25, 1923, the six engine giant set a number of records, including those for weight carrying, altitude with a load, and flight duration. The Barling Bomber was designed to demonstrate the utility of extremely large transport aircraft, but flying was limited to the Midwest as it was unable to climb over the Allegheny Mountains.

September 4, 1923—The *Shenandoah* (ZR-1) made its first flight at Lakehurst, N. J. *Shenandoah* was the first airship in the world to employ helium as a lifting gas rather than the explosive hydrogen. The ship's skipper was Lt. Cmdr. Zachary Lansdowne, a native of Greenville, Ohio.

September 6, 1923—Lt. A. F. Hegenberger and Bradley F. Jones, civilian navigator, flew above the clouds from McCook Field to New York, testing new navigation techniques.

October 23, 1923—Frederick Patterson, president of the National Cash Register Company of Dayton, was elected president of the National Aeronautic Association.

1924—McCook Field pilots flew the night airways system between Dayton and Columbus on a regular basis.

March 7, 1924—Lt. E. H. Barksdale and Bradley Jones traveled from McCook Field to Mitchel Field, N.Y., on instruments.

March 1924—Lt. James Doolittle conducted a series of dive stress tests to determine the degree of acceleration combat planes could withstand.

March-April 1924—The first induction compass was developed at McCook Field.

May 2, 1924—Lts. Albert W. Stevens and John Macready climbed to an altitude of 31,540 feet to take a high altitude photograph showing more of the earth's surface than had ever been visible before.

June 18, 1924—Lt. Macready was forced to make the first emergency parachute jump while flying the night airways system.

October 2-4, 1924—The International Air Races were held at Wilbur Wright Field. Events included a variety of races, balloon flights, formation flying, and aerial combat demonstrations by the First Pursuit Group; parachute jumps, skywriting, and a public inspection of the Barling Bomber.

July 1, 1925—Remote control equipment developed by Air Service personnel at McCook Field allowed the pilot of an airplane to manipulate a driverless car moving on the ground.

July 1925—The first radio beacon equipment was installed in a Department of Commerce mail plane. These beacons and other navigational aids were developed at McCook Field.

July 1925—Maj. Jack Berry officially opened Cleveland's 1000 acre, $1,000,000 municipal airport.

September 3, 1925—The rigid airship *Shenandoah*, the "Daughter of the Skies," crashed near Ava, Ohio. Cmdr. Lansdowne and 13 crew members were lost as the ship broke up during a storm encountered while touring the Midwest. When souvenir hunters who swarmed to the site threatened to strip the craft of objects necessary in determining the cause of the crash, federal officials were forced to declare martial law in the area.

October 21, 1925—Lt. James H. Doolittle of the flight test branch of McCook Field won the Schneider Cup seaplane race in a Curtiss airplane.

1925—Lt. George W. Goddard of the photographic section at McCook Field developed a lighting technique which made night photography possible. Among the first night photos ever taken were pictures of Springfield and Dayton, Ohio, and Rochester, N. Y.

January 29, 1926—John Macready set a world altitude record of 38,704 feet in an XCO5-A at McCook Field.

February 12, 1926—Art Williams, a well-known speed flyer, died in a crash at Montpelier, Ohio.

May 12, 1926—Lincoln Ellsworth, whose boyhood home was Hudson, Ohio, flew across the North Pole in the dirigible *Norge*. Ellsworth and Roald Amundsen, the Norwegian explorer who had been first to reach the South Pole, had attempted a polar crossing previously in two Dornier-Wal flying boats, but had been forced down on the polar ice cap 150 miles short of their goal. After a month on the ice, they had succeeded in repairing their planes and returning to Spitsbergen, Norway. The pair secured the *Norge* and the services of her Italian commander, Umberto Nobile, for their second assault on the pole. Their dreams of being the first to fly over the roof of the world were dashed when Cmdr. Richard E. Byrd and his crew in a Fokker monoplane completed the flight on May 9. However, Ellsworth and Amundsen decided to make the flight in spite of Byrd's coup. Departing from Spitsbergen, they landed in Teller, Alaska, after a flight of 3393 miles.

1926—Thompson Products Incorporated was officially adopted as the name of the Cleveland firm founded by Charles E. Thompson. Originally known as the Electric Welding Company and later as the Steel Products Corporation, the company's most important contribution to aeronautical progress was the development of improved valves for aircraft engines. Thompson entered the field in 1904 with the manufacture of valves for Winton automobiles. By 1926 the firm's hollow, salt-cooled valves were standard equipment on American engines.

July 18, 1926—The *Pilgrim*, Goodyear's revolutionary semirigid airship, was launched at Akron. Frequently referred to as "America's first air yacht," the ship boasted a luxuriously appointed passenger cabin with mahogany paneling and blue mohair seats. The *Pilgrim* was the first American airship to have the cabin completely enclosed and rigged flush with the gasbag. By the time of its retirement on December 30, 1931, the *Pilgrim* had carried 5355 passengers over a total of 94,974 miles.

April 1927—The 87th General Assembly appointed a committee to study the problems of commercial aviation in Ohio and recommend legislation to regulate the state's air traffic.

May 21, 1927—Charles A. Lindbergh made the first solo, nonstop flight from New York to Paris. *The Spirit of St. Louis* was equipped with valves, propeller, tubing, motor forgings, and paint manufactured by Ohio corporations. Upon landing in Paris, the "Lone Eagle" was met by the ambassador to France, Myron T. Herrick, a native of Huntington, Ohio.

October 10, 1927—Continental Airlines of Cleveland received airmail contracts for Cleveland, Akron, Dayton, Columbus, Cincinnati, and Louisville.

October 12, 1927—Wright Field was formally dedicated as the new U. S. Army Air Corps engineering test center. Short runways, crowded shop conditions, and the inability to expand had forced officials of the Air Corps (the former Air Service) to select a site to replace McCook Field. The new facility was opened with impressive ceremonies which included appearances by national figures and a massive flyby demonstration of American air might.

February 3, 1928—Lt. H. A. Sutton of Wright Field began a series of aircraft spin tests for which he was later awarded the McKay Trophy.

February 18, 1928—The Parker brothers erected a hangar at the airport in Sandusky. On January 29, 1929, the brothers made the first flight to Kelleys Island and on November 29, 1931, inaugurated regular mail service to the Lake Erie islands.

June 16, 1928—Tests were made of a new supercharger designed to supply sea level air pressure to aircraft engines at 30,000 feet. Wright Field engineers were also developing a liquid oxygen system for crews flying at high altitudes.

August 1, 1928—Continental Airlines opened passenger service from Cleveland to Louisville, Ky.

October 10, 1928—Capt. St. Clair Street and Capt. Albert W. Stevens set an altitude record for planes carrying more than one passenger as they climbed to 37,854 feet over Wright Field.

October 18, 1928—Fred Lund, flying a WACO at Troy, flew the first successful outside loop ever accomplished in a civilian plane.

Fall 1928—The Great Lakes Aircraft Corporation was founded. The company purchased the Martin plant when that company moved from Cleveland to Baltimore. Great Lakes later produced Torpedo bombers for the Navy as well as a fine series of military trainers and light civilian planes.

November 1928—The Aeronautical Corporation of America, a Cincinnati firm, produced the Aeronca, a small, lightweight aircraft which helped popularize "sport" flying.

January 9, 1929—The first Army airplane to be flown to a foreign station, a C-2 transport, traveled from Wright Field to France Field in Central America, with Maj. Paul Bock at the controls.

February 23, 1929—Wright Field scientists announced the development of special high altitude gloves and goggles and an oxygen heating system which permitted extended flights in the substratosphere.

March 1929—David Ingalls, member of the Ohio house of representatives from Cuyahoga County, introduced the state's first bill regulating civil aeronautics. The act created an Ohio Aviation Board to govern the creation of airports and new air routes, as well as to set safety standards for aircraft operating in Ohio. John Vorys was named first director of the new agency.

June 14, 1929—Cleveland became a terminal on the first air-rail transcontinental passenger service.

August 28, 1929—The National Air Races were held in Cleveland for the first time. The races, which were destined to become an annual showplace for American aviation, featured Charles A. Lindbergh flying with the Navy "High Hats," a precision acrobatic team; Amelia Earhart demonstrating glider techniques, and Juan DeCierva's autogyro. An airplane which was released from the airship *Los Angeles* circled and returned to the mother ship while still in flight. Lt. Adolphus Groton became the first man to transfer from a rigid airship to an airplane in flight. The Mitchell Trophy, a speed trophy for military pilots, was awarded to Lt. Paul Wortswith. The Thompson Trophy, which was to become the classic American speed trophy, was won by Doug Davis of Atlanta, Ga., who won the 50 mile pylon event.

November 7, 1929—Rear Adm. William A. Moffett, chief of the Navy Bureau of Aeronautics, drove a rivet into the main ring of the ZR-4 at the christening of the *Akron*, named in honor of the city in which it was constructed. The potential of the Zeppelin for naval reconnaissance was one of the most striking features of aeronautical development to emerge from the First World War. Following the war the United States acquired one Zeppelin, the ZR-3, *Los Angeles*, as part of German reparations payments. A second, the *Shenandoah*, was constructed at the Philadelphia Naval Yard based on the plans of a Zeppelin captured during the war. By the fall of 1923 conditions in Germany had become so unsettled that the Goodyear Tire and Rubber Company of Akron, which had been manufacturing both free sport balloons and tethered observation craft, was able to persuade the Luftshiffbau Zeppelin Company of Germany to form a partnership in which Goodyear would hold two-thirds of the stock. Key members of the engineering staff, headed by Dr. Karl Arnstein, were transferred to Akron to form the scientific and design base of the new Goodyear-Zeppelin Corporation. In addition, Goodyear gained control of all North American patents held by the old Luftshiffbau company. The Goodyear airship dock, a huge hangar to house the giant craft during construction, was built. This building remained the largest structure in the world without internal supports until the construction of the Houston Astrodome.

November 6, 1930—Edward V. Rickenbacker, America's Ace of Aces, was awarded the Congressional Medal of Honor for action on September 25, 1918.

1930—By the fourth decade of the century, Ohio had become the nation's aeronautical capital. There were 576 airplanes registered in the state, with 690 pilots and 505 mechanics licensed under state law.

May 1931—The last Army Air Corps maneuvers held between the wars took place at the Fairfield Air Depot under the direction of Gen. B. D. Foulois. An aerial armada of 660 airplanes of all types was assembled to take part in a series of formation flights and cross country bombing and interception practices.

July 1931—Patterson Field near Fairfield was named for Frank Stuart Patterson, a World War I pilot who had been killed while testing aircraft at Wilbur Wright Field in 1919. The new field was comprised of the former Wilbur Wright Field and the Fairfield Air Depot.

August 31, 1931—The National Air Races returned to Cleveland. Mrs. Phoebe Omlie won the women's division of the Transcontinental Air Tour; Lowell Bayles won the Thompson Trophy in a Granville brothers Gee-Bee; James Doolittle won the Bendix Trophy in a Laird Solution racer.

1931—Maj. Gen. Malcolm Grow began studying the ideal psychophysical human structure for combat flying, at Wright Field.

James H. Doolittle after he won the first Bendix Trophy race in 1931 in the National Air Races at Cleveland.

May 9, 1932—Lt. Alfred Hegenberger made the first solo instrument landing in history at Wright Field.

August 27-September 5, 1932—The National Air Races were held in Cleveland again. James G. Haizlip established a transcontinental record of 10 hours, 19 minutes to win the Bendix Trophy. Mrs. Mae Haizlip flew her husband's Wedell-Williams racer to a new land speed record for women of 252.513 miles per hour. James Doolittle, in a Gee-Bee Supersportster, won the Thompson Trophy with a speed of 252.68 miles per hour. Doolittle also broke the world's speed record as he flew the Gee-Bee at 294 miles per hour over the three kilometer course in Cleveland on September 3.

January 1933—Ernst Loebell, a German engineer living in Cleveland, founded the Cleveland Rocket Society, the second such group in the nation. A graduate of the University of Oldenburg in power engineering, Loebell while still in Germany had become interested in the work of the Romanian rocket theorist, Hermann Oberth, and had joined the Verein für Raumschiffahrt, an embryonic group conducting experiments with liquid fuel rocket engines. Loebell carried his interest in rocketry with him when he moved to Cleveland in 1930, and, with the help of E. L. Hanna, member of a prominent Cleveland family, he was able to organize a small group of

James Wedell in the Wedell-Williams racer, just after finishing second in the 1932 Bendix race at Cleveland.

enthusiasts. In spite of criticism which appeared in the local press and constant financial problems, the Cleveland rocket group constructed six engines and carried out a basic program of experimentation. In 1936, the French government invited the society to submit a rocket for the International Exposition of 1937. A 35 foot aluminum rocket with instruments, engine, and recovery apparatus was sent to Paris, but no flights were made. Lack of financial support and trained personnel to assist Loebell were the primary reasons for the society's dissolution in 1938.

March 11, 1933—Adm. Moffett's wife christened the ZR-5, *Macon*, in the airship dock at Akron. *Macon*, the second major airship constructed by the Goodyear-Zeppelin Corporation, was designed to serve as a scout vehicle for the American fleet. She was equipped to carry a number of airplanes, launch them, and retrieve them as well as service them when necessary. Properly utilized, this type of aircraft could have made *Macon* an indispensable scouting aid to fleet officers. The airship made four trial flights from the Akron hangar between April 21 and June 14, the longest of which was a 48 hour tour of Wisconsin, Illinois, and Michigan.

April 4, 1933—The *Akron* was lost in a violent storm off Little Egg Inlet, N. J. Of the 76 crew members, only Lt. Cmdr. Herbert Wiley, the ship's navigator; AM Moody Erwin, and BM Richard E. Deal survived. Adm.

William A. Moffett, chief of the Navy Bureau of Aeronautics and patron of the rigid airship program, died in the crash. The blimp J-3 was lost searching for survivors.

September 1933—Roscoe Turner won the Bendix Trophy at the National Air Races in Cleveland. James Wedell won the Thompson Trophy in the Wedell-Williams racer, and Al Williams won the Phillips Trophy with a world speed record of 305.33 miles per hour.

Lt. Cmdr. Thomas G. W. Settle and Maj. Chester Fordney aloft on the first American stratosphere balloon flight, November 21, 1933.

November 21, 1933—Lt. Cmdr. Thomas G. W. Settle and Maj. Chester Fordney set a balloon altitude record of 61,237 feet on a flight from Akron. Settle, a Navy balloon inspector at the Goodyear plant, had had extensive experience as a balloonist before being approached by Auguste Piccard, the famous French stratospheric balloonist and diver, to pilot the *Century of Progress*, a high altitude research balloon with a sealed, pressurized gondola, at the Century of Progress Exposition in Chicago. Settle was able to make one flight from Soldier Field, Chicago, August 4, 1933, but cut it short when the gas valve stuck open soon after takeoff. Upon his landing, the crowd witnessing the event became unruly, rushed to the balloon, and began to tear off large sections of the fabric as souvenirs. After repairs were made to the balloon and gondola, it was decided to transfer the flight to the Goodyear airship dock in Akron, where it was possible to keep the crowd at a distance. The craft was inflated and the gondola rigged to the gasbag inside the hangar, so that when the weather became favorable, the flight could begin immediately. During the initial stages of the ascent on November 21, Settle perched on top of the gondola, checking the lines and instruments. By 12:45 p.m., as Settle and Fordney passed over East Liverpool, the hatches were sealed and they began an examination of the instruments. Although they hoped to break the world altitude record of 60,695 feet recently set by Russian aeronauts, the primary purpose of the flight was to gather cosmic ray data and meteorological information in the upper atmosphere. The balloon traveled across the eastern United States, coming to earth near Bridgeton, N. J., at 5:50 p.m.

1934—The first airport landing traffic control system was installed at Hopkins Airport, Cleveland, by Maj. Jack Berry and Claude King.

August 4-5, 1934—At the Women's National Air Races in Dayton, Arlene Davis of Lakewood, Ohio, was the winner. Miss Davis later became the first woman to hold a multiengine pilot's rating, and was the only woman to instruct male flying cadets in instrument techniques during World War II.

September 15, 1934—Maj. Gen. Harry G. Armstrong was assigned to special research projects in the area of aeromedical studies for the Air Corps at Wright Field.

September 1934—In the National Air Races at Cleveland, Douglas Davis, flying a Wedell-Williams racer, won the Bendix Trophy. Roscoe Turner set a new coast-to-coast record of 10 hours, 2 minutes, and 51 seconds. Turner also captured the Thompson Trophy with a record speed of 248.12 mph.

February 12, 1935—The ZR-5, *Macon*, was lost off Point Sur, Calif., ending an era in American aeronautical history. The top vertical fin, which had been damaged in a Texas storm, gave way, making the *Macon* difficult to control and eventually forcing Cmdr. Herbert Wiley, her skipper, to land in the Pacific. Unlike the *Shenandoah* and *Akron* disasters, the death toll was low, with only two of the *Macon*'s crew lost. The end of the *Macon* provided enemies of the rigid airship with ammunition which they used to bring to an end the construction of these "giants of the sky."

The "Daughter of the Skies," *Shenandoah* (ZR-1), rides at the mooring mast at Lakehurst, N. J.

August 20, 1935—Leslie Tower and a crew composed of Air Corps personnel and Boeing employees died in the crash of the experimental Boeing 299 at Wright Field. This craft was the prototype of the B-17 of World War II fame.

January 1936—Ernest C. Hall, a native of Warren, Ohio, was appointed assistant state director of aeronautics by Gov. Martin L. Davey, and was promoted to head of the department soon thereafter. Hall had built and flown his first airplane, a Bleriot type, as early as 1911. In 1915 he purchased a Wright Model G flying boat with which he established the Hall Flying School at Conneaut Lake, Pa. On December 15, 1915, he accepted a position as civilian flight instructor with the U. S. Army Signal Corps. Remaining in this position throughout World War I, he served at Wilbur Wright Field and later as chief flight instructor at Call Field, Texas. During his three years with the Bureau of Aeronautics he took an active part in all Ohio air meets, investigated air crashes, suggested regulatory legislation, and was instrumental in the selection of sites for new airports. Hall is the oldest living flight instructor and pilot in the nation, having been actively engaged in flying for more than 60 years. He still instructs students at his flying school at Warren, Ohio.

February 11, 1936—Iona Coppedge and Josephine Garrigus set a woman's altitude record of 15,252.579 feet in an Aeronca over Dayton.

1937—The Taylor Aircraft Corporation in Alliance was reorganized. The new corporation, Taylor-Young, produced the famous Taylorcraft airplanes.

The pride of the fleet, the *Akron* (ZR-4), hovers over a crowd at Lakehurst, N. J.

April 23, 1937—Capt. Carl Crane, Capt. George Holloman, and Raymond Stout made the first fully automatic landing in history at Wright Field.

August 5, 1937—The XC-35, the Air Corps' first experimental pressurized cabin airplane, was tested at Wright Field.

September 1937—The National Air Races drew record crowds in Cleveland. The Bendix Trophy was awarded to Frank Fuller, who flew from Los Angeles to Cleveland in 7 hours, 54 minutes. Rudy Kling won the Thompson Trophy with an average speed of 256.91 mph. Crowds thrilled to the stunt flying and parachute events as well as the precision flying of the Navy squadrons. Lee Miles of Fort Worth, Texas, lost his life in a crash during the races.

December 9, 1937—Cleveland was awarded a five year contract to hold the National Air Races in the city.

March 22, 1938—Edward V. Rickenbacker purchased Eastern Airlines for $3,500,000.

September 1938—In the National Air Races at Cleveland, the Bendix Trophy was awarded to Jacqueline Cochran, who flew her Seversky fighter nonstop, Los Angeles to Mitchel Field on Long Island, N. Y., in 8 hours, 10 minutes, 31 seconds. The hit of the Air Races, however, was Douglas "Wrong Way" Corrigan, who flew to Cleveland in the Curtiss Robin in which he had flown from New York to Dublin. Roscoe Turner won the Thompson Trophy in his Laird Solution racer.

1939—Akron Aircraft Corporation was founded to produce a light, two place monoplane. Culver Aircraft was founded in Columbus. WACO built a series of airplanes for the Brazilian Air Force.

July 30, 1939—The Boeing B-15 set a world payload-carrying record as it climbed to 8200 feet over Wright Field with a 15 and one-half ton payload.

September 1939—Roscoe Turner became the only pilot to win the Thompson Trophy three times as he flew his Laird racer at an average speed of 282.536 mph. Frank Fuller in a Seversky fighter won the Bendix Trophy for the second time.

1939—Dr. Jason J. Nassau designed the large telescope built by Warner and Swasey for the Warner and Swasey Observatory of the Case School of Applied Science. This instrument permitted astronomers to photograph several thousand stars at once and conduct spectroscopic studies of the heavens.

1940—The National Advisory Committee for Aeronautics established its major propulsion laboratory in Cleveland. Initial studies undertaken at the center included experiments with reciprocating engines and jet power plants. In 1942 a wind tunnel capable of recreating conditions at altitudes up to 50,000 feet and speeds up to 400 mph was constructed. In 1947 the laboratory was named the George W. Lewis Flight Propulsion Laboratory. During this period NACA scientists explored the problems of supersonic flight and rocket power.

June 1941—Col. Donald J. Keirn of Wright Field was sent to England to study the Gloucester jet and engine developed by Frank Whittle, an English engineer.

May 17, 1942—Wright Field was the terminus of the first cross-country helicopter flight in history.

1945—Capt. Don S. Gentile of Piqua was Ohio's leading World War II ace with a total of 30 kills. Following Capt. Gentile's death in 1950 in a T-33 jet trainer crash at Andrews Air Force Base, Md., the Defense Supply Center in Dayton was renamed for him. First Lt. John Voll, a native of Goshen, Ohio, was the top-ranking ace of the 15th Air Force with 21 kills to his credit.

February 3, 1946—Army Air Force officials in Columbus announced the development of an airplane which would take off, fly, and land under the control of preset radio equipment.

April 24, 1946—The world's first glider freight service was instituted as a WACO glider was towed from Philadelphia to San Juan, Puerto Rico, by a DC-3.

August 17, 1946—Sgt. Larry Lambert of Wright Field became the first man to eject from an aircraft in flight. The jump was part of an Air Force program seeking new methods of escape from high speed aircraft.

August 30, 1946—Paul Mantz won the first postwar Bendix Trophy, averaging 435.604 mph. Alvin M. Johnson was awarded the Thompson Trophy in the reciprocating engine class, while the jet class trophy went to Maj. Gus Lundquist, flying a Lockheed P-80. In view of the increasing speeds possible with jet aircraft, the traditional Thompson Trophy was divided into two classes—civilians competing in the reciprocating class, and military fliers vying for the new jet class trophy.

August 30-September 2, 1946—Ohioan Cook Cleland won the Thompson Trophy flying a Navy Corsair. The Bendix Trophy went to Paul Mantz who averaged 460.423 mph in a P-51.

October 1, 1946—The *Truculent Turtle*, a Navy P2V patrol bomber, set a world nonstop distance flying record as it traveled from Perth, Australia, to Columbus, Ohio. The plane covered 11,822 miles in a little over 55 hours of continuous flying.

November 15-24, 1946—The National Air Show was held in Cleveland.

September 21, 1947—An Air Force C-54, equipped with robot flying equipment and an automatic pilot, flew from Clinton County Air Force Base, Wilmington, Ohio, to Brize Norton, England, and returned under automatic control.

January 30, 1948—Orville Wright, age 76, died in Dayton following a collapse in his laboratory.

January 1948—The huge Air Force installations at Wright and Patterson fields were merged to become Wright-Patterson Air Force Base. On June 8, 1948, a 10,000 foot runway, the longest man-made runway in the world, was officially opened.

April 27, 1949—The Sikorsky A-52-1 helicopter was flown to a new world speed record of 129.6 mph by Harold Thompson in Cleveland.

June 17, 1952—Goodyear delivered the ZPN-1, the world's largest non-rigid airship, to the Navy.

July 15-31, 1952—The first helicopter crossing of the Atlantic was completed by Harry C. Jeffers of Newark and Harold Moore of Cincinnati. Piloting Sikorsky H-19 helicopters, they flew from Westover Air Force Base, Mass., to Prestwick, Scotland, in 42 hours, 35 minutes flying time.

September 1953—The National Air Show was held at Cox Municipal Airport, Vandalia, Ohio. On September 2, Capt. Russell Dobyns flew a Piaseki YH-21 helicopter to a record altitude of 22,289 feet. Flying the same machine on September 5, Dobyns set a three kilometer speed record of 146.735 mph. Brig. Gen. Stanley Holtoner, flying an F-86D, set a speed mark of 690.18 mph over a 100 kilometer course, while Capt. Harold Collins flew his Sabrejet to a speed of 707.889 mph over a 15 kilometer course. The Bendix Trophy was awarded to Maj. William Whisner, Jr., who flew an F-86 from Muroc Dry Lake, Calif., to Vandalia in 3 hours, 5 minutes, and 45 seconds.

November 3, 1954—The National Air Races returned to Cox Municipal Airport. Capt. Edward W. Kinney won the Bendix Trophy in an F-86 with an average speed of 616.208 mph. Capt. Harold Collins set a world speed record of 649.302 mph on a 500 kilometer closed course.

November 13, 1956—Maj. Arnold Beck soared to 198,770 feet in an Air Research and Development Command altitude chamber at Wright-Patterson Air Force Base.

August 15, 1958—T. Keith Glennan, president of Case Institute of Technology, Cleveland, was named by Pres. Dwight Eisenhower as the first administrator of the newly-created National Aeronautics and Space Administration, successor to the National Advisory Committee for Aeronautics. As administrator, Glennan was responsible for the establishment of the basic goals of the American space effort. The first tentative steps toward the moon, including the launching of the nation's first earth satellites and the planning of Project Mercury, which would carry the first American into space, were taken during Dr. Glennan's term as administrator, 1958-1961.

Under NASA auspices, space research carried out at the Lewis Flight Propulsion Laboratory, Cleveland, included designing the control system and capsule for Project Mercury, development of the rocket engine to power the X-15 high altitude research craft, accumulation and analysis of high speed wind tunnel data used in the design of the XB-70, and development of high energy fuel sources to power the Saturn rocket which would carry man to the moon.

April 1959—Col. John H. Glenn of New Concord, Ohio, was selected as one of the original seven Project Mercury astronauts. Glenn, a Marine Corps aviator, had earlier become the first man to fly coast to coast faster than the speed of sound. Much of the early planning for the project, including that for many of the rigorous physical and psychological examinations, was conducted in Ohio, both at Wright-Patterson Air Force Base and at the Lewis Flight Propulsion Laboratory in Cleveland. Several major Ohio corporations made contributions to Project Mercury. The B. F. Goodrich Company of Akron developed the space suits which protected our first astronauts. Russell Colley, a Goodrich researcher, pioneered in the field of life support systems for high altitude pilots. As early as 1933, he produced the first flight pressure suit for Wiley Post's round the world flight. A similar model produced for Post in 1934 enabled him to reach an altitude of 47,000 feet in his famous Lockheed Vega, *Winnie Mae*. The company gained additional experience in the field by producing the series of altitude suits worn by American pilots and air crews during the 1950's and 1960's. One of the major problems faced by those planning Project Mercury was the tremendous heat which any spacecraft would encounter during reentry into the earth's atmosphere. The Cincinnati Testing and Research Company found the solution in the development of the ablative heat shield, composed of ceramic materials which flaked off during reentry, thus dissipating the heat.

December 31, 1959—A B-47 returned to Wright-Patterson Air Force Base after having flown 49,200 miles for a nonstop distance record.

May 23, 1961—A large wind tunnel capable of recreating conditions at Mach 14 (14 times the speed of sound) at altitudes up to 200,000 feet and temperatures as high as 2500° F. was installed at Wright-Patterson Air Force Base.

December 20, 1961—Neil Armstrong, a NASA civilian test pilot, flew an extremely successful mission in the high speed, high altitude test craft, X-15. Armstrong, a native of Wapakoneta, had taken an early interest in aircraft and astronomy. He earned his private pilot's license at the age of 16, some months before he learned to drive an automobile. At Purdue University he worked toward a degree in aeronautical engineering until his college career was interrupted by service in the Navy during the Korean War. Following Navy service and completion of his college training, Armstrong attended the test pilot school at the flight research center conducted by the Air Force and the National Aeronautics and Space Administration at Edwards Air Force Base, Calif.

February 20, 1962—John H. Glenn became the first American to orbit the earth, as he circled the globe three times in his capsule, *Friendship 7*. During the second orbit a warning light informed monitors on the ground that the ablative heat shield, which dissipated capsule heat and protected the astronaut during the fiery reentry period, was no longer locked in position. Ground control decided to retain the retrorocket pack which was normally jettisoned after it had been used to position the capsule for reentry, in the hope that it would help hold the shield in place during the final critical moments of the flight. As Glenn streaked into the upper layers of the atmosphere, the intense heat surrounding the capsule ionized the air, disrupting communications with the ground for the last seven minutes of the flight. In spite of the problems, the mission was brought to a successful conclusion. It demonstrated that a man could function effectively in space under conditions of extreme stress. On March 3, 1962, Glenn was officially welcomed home in New Concord, Ohio. An estimated 50,000 persons crowded into the town of 2127 population.

June 21, 1962—Neil Armstrong was awarded the Octave Chanute Trophy by the Institute of Aerospace Sciences as the pilot who had contributed most to the field during the previous year. On July 17, NASA's director of manned space flight, O. Brainerd Holmes, announced that Armstrong would become the first civilian astronaut to participate in the Gemini and Apollo programs.

August 1962—The Behavioral Sciences Laboratory of Wright-Patterson Air Force Base and the Ford Motor Company began an effort to identify skills which would be required by future members of aerospace flight crews.

August 12, 1962—The Sohio Research Center in Cleveland successfully tracked the flights of the Soviet spacecraft Vostock III and IV.

October 1962—A motion simulator platform, a device which recreates the sensations of space flight, was installed at Wright-Patterson Air Force Base. It was used to test the physical tolerances of astronaut candidates. The Multiple Axis Space Test Inertia Facility, or MASTIF, a device which simulated emergency conditions in space, was installed at the Lewis Flight Propulsion Laboratory in Cleveland. MASTIF tumbled astronaut candidates on three axes simultaneously, at speeds up to 60 rotations per minute, to study their reactions under conditions of extreme vertigo.

October 18, 1963—Ohioan Donn F. Eisele was named to the astronaut training program.

March 19-April 17, 1964—Mrs. Geraldine Mock of Columbus became the first woman to fly around the world solo, covering the 23,103 miles in 29 days, 11 hours, and 55 minutes. Mrs. Mock was also the first woman to solo the Pacific west to east in a single engine aircraft.

1965—Gen. Curtis E. LeMay retired as Air Force chief of staff. A native of Columbus, LeMay began his Air Force career as an ROTC cadet at The Ohio State University. An early exponent of strategic bombing concepts, he was instrumental in the development of navigational techniques for use by combat air crews. During World War II, Gen. LeMay commanded the famed 305th Bomb Group which was involved in some of the most difficult missions of the air war in Europe. In January 1945, he was transferred to the XX Bomber Command, which he led in the fire raids that devastated Japanese industrial capacity. Following the war LeMay served with a number of commands, eventually assuming leadership of the nation's primary deterrent force, the Strategic Air Command. Under his guidance SAC became America's strong right arm, capable of flying combat missions at any time of day or night. Gen. LeMay was appointed vice chief of staff of the Air Force under Gen. Thomas D. White in 1957 and named chief of staff upon Gen. White's retirement in 1961.

December 4-18, 1965—Gemini-Titan 7 carried Command Pilot Frank Borman and Cleveland-born Pilot James A. Lovell, Jr., aloft. Eleven days later Gemini-Titan 6A, with Command Pilot Walter M. Schirra, Jr., and Pilot Thomas P. Stafford aboard, was launched. The two craft achieved the world's first space rendezvous as Gemini 6A climbed into the orbital path of Gemini 7, approaching within six feet of the spacecraft. For five and one-half hours the two flew in formation at distances which varied from 20 to 100 feet. Gemini-Titan 6A was up only two days, but Borman and Lovell splashed down after 14 days in orbit.

Ohio-based companies providing components for the Gemini program included the Brush Beryllium Company of Cleveland, which produced the shingles for the exterior of the spacecraft; the Brush Instruments Division of the Clevite Corporation, manufacturers of instruments used in tests of the capsule and launch systems; the Cincinnati Testing Laboratories Division of the Studebaker Corporation, which tested the ablative heat shield materials; Goodyear Tire and Rubber Company Aerospace Division, producers of the Ballute stabilization system and of the paraglider components initially proposed for use during the course of Project Gemini; Grimes Manufacturing Company of Urbana, manufacturers of the telelight panel for the Gemini spacecraft; the Hartman Electrical Manufacturing Company of Mansfield, producers of the thousands of electrical relays employed in the spacecraft; the A. W. Hecker Corporation, Cleveland, which furnished the machine fittings used in the Gemini capsule, and the

Titanium Manufacturing Corporation of Toronto, suppliers of titanium for the Gemini program. Space suits used during the course of the project were designed and produced by the B. F. Goodrich Company, Akron.

February 28, 1966—Maj. Charles A. Bassett of Dayton, a member of the third group of astronauts selected for the Gemini and Apollo programs, died in the crash of his T-33 at St. Louis.

March 16-17, 1966—Command Pilot Neil Armstrong and Pilot David Scott completed seven orbits on the Gemini-Titan 8 mission. Intended to explore the problems of docking two spacecraft in orbit, the flight produced some of the most harrowing moments in the history of the American space effort. After having completed a perfect linkup with the unmanned Agena booster which had been placed in orbit earlier, the coupled spacecraft began to gyrate uncontrollably. Armstrong was able to disconnect the two, but the violent gyrations continued to spin the Gemini capsule at a rate of one turn per second. Control was regained through the use of small rockets normally reserved for the positioning maneuvers prior to reentry. An immediate splashdown was ordered, which successfully ended the mission in the western Pacific rather than in the Atlantic Test Range, as originally planned.

November 11-15, 1966—Ohioan James Lovell and Edwin E. Aldrin, Jr., manned the Gemini-Titan 12 mission, the last flight in the Gemini program. The aim of this mission was to complete studies demonstrating the feasibility of extravehicular activity in the vacuum of space. Leaving Command Pilot Lovell in the cockpit of the spacecraft, Astronaut Aldrin ventured outside to undertake a number of assigned tasks which included tethering the capsule to an Agena booster, inspecting the capsule, and taking movies of the earth and the capsule, all of which were vital if the United States were to fulfill Pres. Kennedy's promise of a moon landing by 1970. At the conclusion of this flight Astronaut Lovell had logged a total of seven million miles in earth orbit, more than any other human being.

December 1967—Scientists at The Ohio State University announced results of a study on the types of microscopic dust particles which fall from space onto the relatively unpolluted snow of the Antarctic plateau.

May 6, 1968—Astronaut Neil Armstrong was forced to eject from NASA's lunar landing research vehicle. This vertical takeoff and landing craft allows lunar module (or LM) pilots to practice simulated lunar landings. Flying at an altitude of 500 feet over Ellington Air Force Base, Texas, the simulator crashed and burned.

August 1968—Airmen at Wright-Patterson Air Force Base were subjected to daily heat stress tests in an effort to determine the temperatures astronauts could withstand in the event the cabin cooling system failed during reentry. It was discovered that some individuals could undergo temperatures as high as 300° F. for up to 15 to 20 minutes. Aerospace medical experts conducted other tests at Wright-Patterson, including isolation experiments and dietary tests to determine the optimum low residue diet necessary to sustain maximum energy, but produce a minimum of body waste.

October 11, 1968—Commander Walter Schirra, Lunar Module Pilot Walter Cunningham, and Ohio-born Command Module Pilot Donn F. Eisele flew the first successful manned Apollo mission, Apollo 7. In addition to providing checks on the spacecraft and the worldwide network of tracking stations, the mission showed how crews functioned in the new vehicles designed for the program. Schirra, Cunningham, and Eisele were garbed in individual space capsules in the form of 57 pound, $100,000 space suits made of the fireproof, fiber glass material known as Betacloth, manufactured by the Owens-Corning Fiberglas Corporation of Toledo, Ohio. The trio was the first to beam live television pictures to earth from a spacecraft in orbit; the first to fly with the unique Apollo fuel cells, which produce the water consumed by crew members, and the first to suffer head colds in orbit. NASA officials labeled the mission and the equipment which it tested "101 percent perfect."

October 1968—Scientists at the Jet Propulsion Laboratory, Pasadena, Calif., and The Ohio State University announced the successful completion of high altitude tests of a balloon-borne spectrometer. The device was designed to measure radiation levels in the upper atmosphere over a long period of time.

December 21-27, 1968—Apollo 8 carried Commander Frank Borman, Lunar Module Pilot William Anders, and Ohioan James Lovell, the command module pilot, into lunar orbit for the first time. The launch vehicle, the Saturn V, stood 363 feet tall and was composed of three major stages and an interstage, all of which were designed to lift the command, lunar, and service modules into earth orbit. At 11.5 minutes after lift-off, this multimillion dollar vehicle, tall as a 36 story building, completed its task as it deposited the three voyagers in position for their trip.

The flight of Apollo 8 marked a major event in the history of man's conquest of the unknown. Previously, he had remained a prisoner of his planet. Now, for the first time, he ventured forth to inspect his nearest celestial neighbor from an altitude of 70 miles. Like its predecessors, Apollo 8 was designed essentially to test the performance of all Apollo systems prior to a moon landing. The photographs of the surface of the moon and of the earth as it appears from one-quarter of a million miles in space, which were beamed back to earth on Christmas Eve, will remain among the most awe-inspiring ever seen, because, for the first time, a man was holding the camera. After ten revolutions about the moon, the vehicle's propulsion system was restarted to begin the journey home. A failure at this point would have left the trio stranded forever in lunar orbit. Astronaut Lovell's happy quip, "Please be informed there is a Santa Claus," announced to an anxious world that the crew of Apollo 8 was on its way home.

January 13, 1969—The last XB-70, a supersonic research craft used in studies to determine the feasibility of a supersonic commercial transport plane, was flown to Wright-Patterson Air Force Base, where it was added to the flight craft collection of the U. S. Air Force Museum. Established after World War I as a collection of airframes, engines, instruments, and other flight equipment which could be used by engineers in solving aeronautical problems, the Air Force Museum has grown to become one of the largest and finest collections of its kind in the world.

July 16-24, 1969—Command Pilot Neil Armstrong, Command Module Pilot Michael Collins, and Lunar Module Pilot Edwin Aldrin fulfilled man's oldest dream as they guided Apollo 11 on its epoch journey to the moon. At 9:32 a.m. EDT July 16, the five main stage boosters clustered at the base of the giant Saturn V were fired, propelling the three astronauts into space at a speed of 6000 miles per hour. Following the burn of the second stage and separation, the third stage engine was fired for two minutes, raising the spacecraft to an altitude of 115 miles above the earth's surface. A second third stage burn increased the rocket's speed and sent it on its way to a rendezvous with the moon. Once en route, *Columbia*, the command module, separated from the third stage which had borne it aloft, turned on its axis, and docked nose to nose with *Eagle*, the lunar module. After a journey of 239,000 miles, braking rockets were fired to drop the two craft into lunar orbit. Armstrong and Aldrin squeezed through the narrow hatch leading to the LM. This module was the world's first true spacecraft, designed to function solely in the vacuum beyond the earth's protective atmosphere. The crew compartment was much smaller than that of *Columbia* and the usable space of only 160 cubic feet was banked by the computers, instruments, and controls with which the astronauts guided the LM to the lunar surface and back to the waiting command module.

Armstrong and Aldrin began their descent to the moon by firing rockets to slow the LM after its separation from the CM. The LM's primary guidance and navigation system carried the tiny craft to an altitude of 500 feet from the surface, at which point Armstrong took control of the landing maneuvers, slowly turning the LM in order to view the surface of the Sea of Tranquility through the windows on the side. Discovering that the planned landing area was strewn with large boulders, Armstrong set his craft down on a site northwest of the primary area. The final descent was made at a speed of three feet per second. Moments before touchdown, the five foot landing wires extending from the base of the landing pads on the LM's legs signaled the pilot to shut down the descent engines, enabling the LM to fall free for the last few feet. On Sunday July 20 at 4:18 p.m. EDT, Armstrong reported the successful completion of this delicate maneuver with a laconic, "Houston, Tranquility Base here. The *Eagle* has landed."

Prior to beginning the period of extravehicular activity, the two astronauts ran through extensive checklists to insure that the LM was ready to leave the surface of the moon at a moment's notice. The men then depressurized their tiny cockpit and opened the hatch. Armstrong backed through the hatch and onto the "front porch," then stepped onto the ladder attached to the leg of the LM and down to the landing pad at the base of the leg. At 10:56 p.m. EDT, with 109 hours, 24 minutes, and 20 seconds of mission time elapsed, Neil A. Armstrong of Wapakoneta, Ohio, became the first human being to set foot on a truly foreign body as he stepped from the LM's base to the surface of the moon, remarking, "That's one small step for a man, one giant leap for mankind." Immediately he began to gather contingency samples of lunar soil in the vicinity of the spacecraft so that, in the event that an emergency occurred, some samples of this material would be available.

Aldrin then proceeded out of the cockpit and down the ladder to join his companion. The two unveiled a plaque which would remain on the moon with the descent stage of the LM and erected an American flag, wired to remain unfurled in the lunar vacuum. Television cameras were positioned, and a series of prepared scientific experiments were begun. The solar wind collector, a foil sheet to collect low energy particles emitted by the sun, was set up. It later was returned to earth with the astronauts. They then collected bulk samples of surface material for study by geologists, and erected a laser reflecting mirror to permit scientists to measure the exact distance between the earth and moon for the first time. Finally, a seismometer to measure moonquakes or major shifts in the moon's crust was installed. The first tremors directly related to lunar activities and not to the movement of the astronauts occurred on July 25, when the heat of the rising sun caused minor rock slides in neighboring craters.

The takeoff maneuvers were the most crucial of the mission, for if a malfunction developed at this point, Armstrong and Aldrin would be beyond rescue. Exactly as planned, however, the LM's ascent engine fired, carrying the two moonwalkers in the upper stage of the LM into orbit for a rendezvous with the waiting Command Module Pilot Michael Collins.

One of the mission's few harrowing moments occurred when the uncontrollable movements of the *Eagle* during docking maneuvers disrupted communications with Houston. The crisis was short-lived, and Armstrong and Aldrin were soon reunited with Collins. The trusty *Eagle*, having fulfilled its function, was left to drift forever in space. On July 22 the CM completed a successful burn of its engine behind the moon, placing the craft on a path which would carry it back to earth. On July 24 at 12:50 p.m. EDT, the *Columbia* splashed down in the Pacific Ocean. Man had indeed made his greatest leap, and returned successfully.

"One small step for a man. . . ," July 20, 1969.

Bibliography

Although this bibliography does not include all of the references consulted in the preparation of the *Chronology*, it will serve as a guide for those interested in further reading on a particular event or personality.

General Works
Gurney, Gene: *A Chronology of World Aviation* (New York, 1965)
Josephy, Alvin M., Jr., editor: *The American Heritage History of Flight* (New York, 1962)
Miller, Francis Trevelyan: *The World in the Air* (New York, 1930)
Morris, Lloyd and Smith, Kendall: *Ceiling Unlimited, The Story of American Aviation from Kitty Hawk to Supersonics* (New York, 1953)
Shrader, Welman A.: *Fifty Years of Flight, A Chronicle of the Aviation Industry in America, 1903-1953* (Cleveland, 1953)
U. S. Department of the Air Force: *A Chronology of American Aerospace Events and Personalities* (Washington, D. C., 1959)

Ballooning in Ohio
Baldwin, Munson: *With Brass and Gas: An Illustrated and Embellished Chronicle of Ballooning in the Nineteenth Century* (Boston, 1967)
Crouch, Tom D.: "Thomas Kirkby: Pioneer Aeronaut in Ohio," *Ohio History*, v. 79, no. 1, Winter 1970
Haydon, F. Stansbury: *Aeronautics in the Union and Confederate Armies* (Baltimore, 1941)
Maurer, Maurer: "Richard Clayton, Aeronaut," Historical and Philosophical Society of Ohio *Bulletin*, v. 13, no. 2, April 1955
Milbank, Jeremiah: *The First Century of Flight in America* (Princeton, 1943)
Wingfoot Lighter-Than-Air Society *Bulletin* (Akron, Ohio)

Ohio and the Airship
Allen, Hugh: *The Story of the Airship* (Akron, 1930)
Amundsen, Roald and Ellsworth, Lincoln: *First Crossing of the Polar Sea* (New York, 1927)
Rosendahl, Charles E.: *What About the Airship?* (New York, 1938)
Smith, Richard K.: *The Airships Akron and Macon; Flying Aircraft Carriers of the United States Navy* (Annapolis, 1965)

Early Aeronautics in Ohio
Bilstein, Roger E.: "Putting Aircraft to Work: The First Air Freight," *Ohio History*, v. 76, no. 4, Autumn 1967
Freudenthal, Elsbeth E.: *Flight into History; the Wright Brothers and the Air Age* (Norman, 1949)
Frohman, Charles E.: *Sandusky's Yesterdays* (Columbus, 1968)
Kelly, Fred C.: *The Wright Brothers* (New York, 1943)
Maurer, Maurer: "McCook Field, 1917-1927," *Ohio Historical Quarterly*, v. 67, no. 1, January 1958
Renstrom, Arthur G.: *Wilbur and Orville Wright: A Bibliography* (Washington, D. C., 1968)
Rose, William Ganson: *Cleveland; The Making of a City* (Cleveland, 1950)
Wright, Orville: *How We Invented the Aeroplane* (New York, 1953)
Wright, Wilbur: *The Papers of Wilbur and Orville Wright*, edited by Marvin W. McFarland (New York, 1953)

Astronautics

Grimwood, James M.; Hacker, Barton C.; Vorzimmer, Peter J.: *Project Gemini, Technology and Operations* (Washington, D. C., 1969)

Moore, Patrick: *Moon Flight Atlas* (Chicago, 1969)

Swenson, Loyd S.; Grimwood, James M.; Alexander, Charles C.: *This New Ocean; A History of Project Mercury* (Washington, D. C., 1966)

Tascher, John: "U. S. Rocket Society Number Two: The Story of the Cleveland Rocket Society," *Technology and Culture*, v. 7, no. 1, Winter 1966

Time-Life Records: *To the Moon* (New York, 1969)

U. S. National Aeronautics and Space Administration: Chronologies, published documents, and technical reports (Washington, D. C.)

We Seven, by the Astronauts Themselves (New York, 1962)